FROM BUCHENWALD TO HAVANA

The Life and Opinions of a Socialist Professor

JULIAN MARKELS

EVENING STREET PRESS

DUBLIN, OHIO

Evening Street Press

September, 2012

Dublin, Ohio

Cover: "Malecon Sunrise, Havana," by Fabio Sartori.
An obsolescent Russian Lada lighting its way
into the dawn on Havana's 4-mile seaside
boulevard.

ISBN: 978-1-937347-08-6

Printed in the United States of America

www.eveningstreetpress.com

10 9 8 7 6 5 4 3 2 1

For My Parents

Frieda Wolfberg and Alex Markels

What, then, can the Socialist do, if there is no principle of brotherhood in the Westerner, but, on the contrary, an individualist isolationist instinct which stands aloof and demands its rights with sword in hand? Observing that there is no fraternity around, the Socialist tries to talk fraternity into people. To make rabbit stew, you first of all need a rabbit. But there is no rabbit available, i.e., no nature capable of brotherhood, no nature that believes in brotherhood. The frantic Socialist sets desperately to work on the future fraternity, defining it, calculating its size and weight...and determines in advance the division of earthly wealth....But what kind of fraternity will it be if they divide in advance and determine how much each merits and what each must do?

Fyodor Dostoevsky, *Winter Notes on Summer Impressions.*

It is not a matter of how many kilograms of meat one has to eat, or of how many times a year someone can go to the beach, or how many pretty things from abroad you might be able to buy with present-day wages. It is a matter of making the individual feel more complete, with much more inner wealth and much more responsibility.

Che Guevara, "Socialism and man in Cuba."

I suppose there are a lot of connections between socialism and basketball....But none of them are conscious when I'm on the court...My goal is to increase the odds of success for each player on the floor, but without negating the odds of success for everyone else in the process.

Steve Nash, NBA point guard, quoted by Chuck Klosterman in "The Karl Marx of the Hardwood."

TABLE OF CONTENTS

CHAPTER 1. COMING OF AGE AS AN AMERICAN SOLDIER:

BUCHENWALD CONCENTRATION CAMP, 1945

Now in my ninth decade, I can still remember standing on the deck of a destroyer talking with my buddy Phil Epstein on the night before we were to land in Le Havre. It was a clear windless night in March, 1945, with a few stars shining in the darkness and our breath vaporing inside our overcoat collars as we listened to the waves lapping at the ship. We'd gone up on deck to escape the endless crap game going on down below, but we were also feeling something momentous about this evening in our lives, and for that we needed to be outdoors. We could see before us in dark outline the shore of Europe, we talked a little about how we might never come back, and that led us to talk again, as we had talked often before, about the meaning of the war.

Phil was a Communist, like thousands of Americans who fought in this war. He believed that Nazism, with the hatred and destruction it spawned, was a natural and necessary outgrowth of capitalism. Like the rest of us, he was risking his life to save Europe from the Nazis, but he also had a larger vision of saving humanity from capitalism's long-term destructiveness, of which Nazism was for him just one variation facing us tomorrow. Phil reasoned intensely in his soft thin voice, now pointing to the Nazis' sponsorship by corporations like Krups and Thyssen, now to the German people's politics that denied their own humanity, and every so often quoting Marx or Lenin.

Not only had he thought about all this a lot more than I had. He lived in Greenwich Village, and that gave him for me a dazzling aura. Just before crossing the Atlantic to England in February, our 84th Field Hospital had been stationed for six weeks at Fort Dix, New Jersey awaiting a ship. Our training was complete, we were marking time, and we regularly got passes to visit this fabled city where Jews lived comfortably amidst the vibrating street life, museums and bookstores, Broadway and Harlem, restaurants and jazz clubs—a larger, richer, more complete human world than I had known growing up in Chicago. In New York with Phil and Paul Leder, my other New York Jewish buddy, I ate all kinds of food for the unforgettable first time. I gawked in the Metropolitan and in gay bars, I saw highbrow theater and stand-up comics, Leonid Massine's Ballet Russe and Leonard Bernstein's *On The Town*, Duke Ellington in a darkened nightclub, and Union Square orators preaching socialism in broad daylight.

Phil and his communist family felt like an integral part of all this. I was 19 years old, and it seemed as if in all sorts of ways my life had led me in spirit to them in their city. My parents were not working class like Phil's, but middle-class Zionists and liberals, also big readers, music lovers, card players, and sports fans (my father). By the time of my Bar Mitzvah in 1938, I'd been going door-to-door in the neighborhood (where I also sold *Cosmopolitan* and *The Ladies Home Companion*) with a little blue tin bank soliciting dimes for the Jewish National Fund—trying to fill my quota for the synagogue where I went daily to Hebrew School and also belonged to Boy Scout Troop #34. My parents belonged to the Committee on Soviet-American Friendship, my father to the National Lawyers' Guild (a still functioning liberal alternative to the American Bar Association), and my mother to a women's book club conducted by a deeply learned woman who I found out years later was also a communist. My parents subscribed to George Seldes' *In Fact*, which reported news suppressed not only by our *Chicago Tribune* but also *The New York Times*, and when I entered the US army they gave me a subscription to *The Nation*.

There was in all of this a side to my growing up that kept me cautious of Phil Epstein's communism. Call it my middle class sense of upwardly mobile privilege. Both my parents were children of immigrants who had struggled to educate themselves and become professionals—my father as an inner city street fighter, second baseman, and shoe salesman who got a night-school law degree from Northwestern, and my mother as a farm town reader at the Carnegie Library who became a crack legal stenographer in

Chicago after graduating from business college in Goshen, Indiana. They aspired to own their own home, with dog, and to send me, my brother Chuck, and my sister Mimi to college. During the 30s they could afford a live-in maid—the physically handicapped daughter of a bankrupt downstate farmer at $5 a week—along with music lessons for us and two weeks of summer camp for me and Chuck. In summer my father also took us to Cubs games at Wrigley Field, and in spring, as a reward for good report cards at school, to the *Chicago Daily News* Relays, where we once saw Glen Cunningham just miss a four-minute mile. My mother made sandwiches for beggars who came to our kitchen door, and we regularly had to Thanksgiving Dinner, along with all the aunts, uncles and cousins, three of the five children of a neighborhood Polish family.

Not that my parents didn't worry about money. My mother was always mending our clothes and inventing new ways to present jello for dessert; she nagged us to turn out the lights when we left a room, and she traipsed from store to store downtown looking for bargains. Bagels with cream cheese and lox, my father's great favorite, were a once-a-month Sunday treat, and when I asked him once how much it would take to make him feel comfortable for his family, he said $10,000 a year would be all he'd ever want—at a time when a first-class postage stamp was 3c, an ice cream cone a nickel, and on Saturdays we could walk two miles to an amusement park and go on five rides for the dime we had made during the week by collecting pop bottles from garbage cans and turning them in for deposit refund. But I don't think we kids ever felt deprived, or denied of opportunity, and in the texture of our lives the opportunity we felt was to become professionally trained, financially secure, culturally enlightened, and politically committed middle class liberals.

In ways that were then obscure to me, this sense of opportunity felt threatened by a commitment like Phil's, as if it might cut me off from the life and world I had some hope of finding. I believe Phil's parents were unionized schoolteachers; they were certainly not upwardly mobile even if they lived in such a fabulous place, and I must have had a sense that my expectations could be larger than Phil's. But neither could I stop thinking about his arguments, or his example, and the six months we now spent in Europe became for me among other things a seedbed of reflection on politics and war.

By dawn the next morning we were in the fabled landing boats we had seen in photographs of the D-Day invasion, and to us they felt like an amusement park ride since we knew we'd be landing safely. Once ashore, we got into trucks that carried us to the eastern edge of the just-ended Battle of the Bulge, a brutal engagement in which the Americans and Germans drove each other back and forth during weeks of daily bloodshed—like *Hamlet*'s Fortinbras fighting the Polacks over a piece of land too small to hold the corpses of those killed. On the way, our truck convoy drove through Liege, and here is another indelible memory: thousands of Belgians lining the boulevards and waving hands, scarves, berets, and babies while cheering us wildly *seven months after D Day!* I felt an immediate, gut-wrenching solidarity with these people, whose gratitude made our presence feel right and necessary.

The convoy took us to a just-cleared minefield outside the village of Chiny, the second-smallest community in Belgium, where we set up our hospital. A field hospital was then the first complete medical installation behind the front lines—with bed wards, x-ray machines, operating rooms, and pharmacy all in long rectangular tents—and also highly mobile. We constantly practiced setting up and taking down the entire hospital in two-and-a-half hours, and we were also subdivided into three units, roughly equivalent to infantry platoons, each fully equipped and independently deployable--three sets of pharmaceuticals, three sets of surgical instruments, cooking pots, etc., all packed in heavy wooden crates with hinged tops. Every enlisted man—pharmacist, x-ray technician, truck driver, cook—was also a stevedore when it came to moving the hospital.

We set up our hospital, along with a softball diamond and volleyball court, in the cleared minefield. But for the five weeks we were there we never had a patient. By that time the Americans had driven the Germans back from the Bulge once and for all, and we had nothing to do but stand guard, play softball, write letters home, and sneakily masturbate in the latrines at night until new battle lines formed to the east and we were called up to a new position.

I was a big letter writer, and my letters were long and detailed. All through school I'd done well in English, I'd been sports editor of my high school paper, and during the year in college I got in return for volunteering instead of waiting to be drafted, I'd taken a creative writing class. Writing home gave me a chance to keep at it, and I wrote not only to parents, brother, and sister, but also sporadically to aunts, uncles, old girlfriends, anyone who would listen. I did this my entire time in the army, and by the time I got home I felt pretty confident as a writer. Not that it came easily to me then any more than now. But I was energized by the process, which has become over time a process of thinking by talking to myself through multiple revisions, and for that I owe the United States Army an unexpected debt.

At this point Phil Epstein disappears from my memory, and I'm not sure why. Nobody in the 84th died in the war, we remained intact as a unit until we were discharged at home a year later, and all I've kept of Phil these 60 years is that night on the destroyer off Le Havre. Maybe it's because his spindly body and total lack of co-ordination unsuited him for sports. I was a beefy, awkward kid who'd always had to struggle for the peer acceptance that only sport could give a Jew where I grew up, and Phil would have been a huge embarrassment on any softball team. Or maybe I felt so guilty for holding out against his communist arguments that I repressed his memory.

Meanwhile, another communist crops up in memory from our weeks in Chiny. Paul Leder found an elderly couple in town who had a short-wave radio. The husband was a woodcutter in the forest from dawn to dark, and in exchange for listening in his house to the war news in English while he ate his supper of egg and potato, we brought them tobacco and candy from our rations. Over several weeks we learned enough French to converse for five minutes, and when one night while talking about winning the peace he blurted out "*Je suis communist*" so as to distinguish himself from his bourgeois son-in-law, the town butcher, I understood not only his words but also how they could express his life.

We played a lot of softball in that minefield, and some of us got serious about volleyball just for variety. We got good enough at it (in the simple way the game was then played) to enter an army-wide tournament, and this enabled us to relieve some of our boredom by traveling to play other teams. We ended up winning the championship of General Bradley's 9th Army, and thirty years later as a university English professor, after two loving but broken marriages, I met Robin Bell across the net in our department's Sunday volleyball game. Our romance began with a kill I tried to stuff down her throat, but she is a jock, dug it out for a return, and now after thirty years I'm more in love with her than ever.

So it was that our first weeks of war turned out to be mostly fun and games—the landing boats, the cheering crowds, the sports we'd grown up with, and mostly good battle news on the short wave radio. Then we got orders to move up to a position just outside Weimar, a city I'd heard about even then as a fabled center of German culture and democracy, and I was in the rearguard left behind to take down the hospital while the others moved up immediately.

Dismantling the hospital took our dozen two days instead of two hours, and when we passed through Chiny on our way out the third day, the woodcutter's daughter and town butcher's wife waved me a big goodbye as I sat down in the truck She was a gorgeous blonde, the most beautiful woman we were to see in Europe, and none of my buddies had the least idea how I knew her. They kept ragging me on the road until we reached Aachen, where suddenly our hearts and minds were changed forever. This stately old city had been an epicenter of the Battle of the Bulge, and now the area we drove through was nothing but rubble for block after block in all four directions as far as you could see. I can still visualize the remnant of an apartment house wall, maybe twenty feet long and crumbling toward the ground from maybe ten feet high, as the only sign that this huge expanse of brick and mortar debris had lately been inhabited by people like my parents living ordinary lives.

2.

I can't speak for all 19-year-olds when they first encounter in daylight the landscape of death in war, but I think that for most of us emotionally, two things happen at once. We hurt and we harden. Our hearts are torn by the inhuman ways in which people destroy each other's lives and communities, and we callous to this hurt. You can't function if you let yourself feel it too intensely or too long, you dilute your humanity if you stop feeling it at all, and we all callous in different ways and degrees. Aachen was for me the beginning of a long, tortuous interplay of hurting and hardening, and Aachen turned out to be just a hint of what was coming.

East of Aachen our convoy suddenly stopped, and we jumped off the trucks into the culvert while two forlorn German planes zoomed down and strafed us. Nobody was hit, the Germans were too disheartened to try again, and we got safely to our overnight destination at a 9th Army barrack. That evening after supper—May 8, 1945—we heard the radio broadcast of Winston Churchill announcing victory in Europe, and the next day we arrived at the majestic manor outside Weimar, with its great circular driveway, its halls and huge rooms with 20-foot ceilings, its multiple outbuildings and big attached park, where the rest of our 84th was now handsomely housed. Then the day after that, two days after V-E day, we reached our new assignment, which turned out to be Buchenwald Concentration Camp.

By now the camp had been liberated for a month, and of the 21,000 inmates who'd been found alive, the only ones left were the hundreds still too sick or weak to be sent back to their native countries. We were given a preliminary tour, and my first view was not of these emaciated, jaundiced, grotesque smelly people but of the roll call yard between their former barracks that had also been the camp's cooking area. This yard was now swept clean, with two enormous brass pots (cauldrons really) mounted on stanchions and scrubbed to the point of shining. Emanating from this vacant, antiseptic, open-air space was the most overpowering smell I have ever experienced. It was as if those pots were just then boiling up a soup of potatoes, maggots, fresh feces, and caked sweat. This stench also permeated the empty barracks in which we were shown next how the Buchenwald prisoners slept six or eight on a wooden shelf that was maybe six feet deep, five feet wide, and twenty inches high.

When we then entered the whitewashed crematorium, the putrid smell gave way to another—the dry, nose-searing whiff of human ashes that for eight years running had been carted from this building in tons. Leading down to the doors of the ovens were black metal tracks on which cast-iron wheelbarrows were mounted, and I've been haunted for the rest of my life by the exquisite design of these wheelbarrows. They were quarter-cylinders long enough to hold an adult human body, yet so shallow as to accommodate only bodies that were fully emaciated, and each with two small indentations for the buttocks so as to secure the body from sliding off while being wheeled into the fire.

Finally we were brought to the surviving inmates, who were now housed, each with a full-sized bed and mattress, in the spacious, high-ceilinged quarters formerly occupied by the SS guards and administrators. Here we imbibed a new, milder aroma of decaying live bodies and lingering feces; we saw for the first time how thin people can become while remaining still alive; and for the next few weeks Paul's and my work for ten hours a day as surgical technicians was to administer intravenous glucose and blood plasma as fast as these could be flown into Weimar, the cradle of German humanism, and then trucked five miles to the "Goethe Oak" around which Buchenwald was built.

The intravenous drip was a desperate intervention designed to give the weakest survivors enough strength to arrest, and hopefully to reverse, the momentum of their physical decay. The 84th's mess sergeant was the best I ever saw, and his genius was not only to make mass-cooked food taste really good but also to gather from local sources a surprising variety of nutritious ingredients. He got a bakery up and going to make us dark bread, and for the Buchenwald survivors he cooked soups that were calculated to be tasty and nourishing without being too rich for people in their condition to digest. But as it turned out for many of our bed-ridden, *any* actual food was too rich to digest, and here is another image that has haunted me. When these people were served their meals, they grabbed their spoons and began frantically stuffing themselves—soup slobbered with one hand and bread gobbled with the other—as if even now, weeks after liberation, all this might disappear without warning. Of course, the more

Coming of Age as an American Soldier

compulsively they ate the less they retained, and the round of meal trays was soon followed by a round of bed-pans.

So it was for dozens that their solid meals had to be reduced or eliminated, and the new skill Paul and I had to learn was getting our needles into their veins. We had practiced intravenous injection in our training, but only on plump American veins, and this was something different. As soon as you got the needle in, it poked through the vein's opposite wall, and, to make things worse, we didn't have near enough thin needles and had to fall back on thick ones. I still wince to remember that in my first two days I punctured five or six arms eight or ten times before managing to keep the needle inside the vein. But in the following days Paul and I became really deft at it—and correspondingly calloused. Paul wore a necklace from which a Star of David hung out from his shirt as he bent over to insert the needle, and upon seeing that, many Jewish patients broke into tears even before feeling the needle in its failed insertion. But he had to ignore their joy with their pain and just keep going.

For weeks after being liberated, Buchenwald had been a showplace for military and political leaders (including before we got there Generals Eisenhower, Bradley, and Patton, as well as Eleanor Roosevelt) who came to see first-hand that the rumors they'd heard were true. Among these visitors after we got there was a steady flow of army M.D.'s, and not a single one of these officers who tried could hit those veins the way Paul and I could. Gotcha, Captain!

By one of those accidents through which history is sometimes preserved to us, there is now available a detailed account of Buchenwald's entire operation, including first-hand accounts by survivors at the time they were liberated, produced by the US Army. Once the extent of the horror became known, the Army assigned a team to document the camp's history, organization, and activities while the evidence was still fresh and before the survivors were dispersed. The report produced by this team within five weeks of liberation was then lost in Army archives for 50 years before being rediscovered and published in 1995 as *The Buchenwald Report*. I have begun reading this book twice and was unable to continue, but now I have culled it enough to make the following summary.

On May 9, 1945, the day my group arrived at the camp, General Bradley sent the following cable to European Theater Headquarters:

> Buchenwald concentration camp has been cleaned up, the sick segregated and burials completed to such an extent that very little evidence of atrocities remains.
>
> This negatives [sic] any educational value of having various groups visit the camp to secure first hand information of German atrocities. In fact, many feel quite skeptical that previous conditions actually existed.

Among the "previous conditions" about whose actual existence many felt skeptical were the following. During Buchenwald's existence from October 1, 1937 to April 11, 1945, 238, 980 prisoners from more than 30 countries were admitted to the camp, and an estimated 34, 566 either died, or were shot, or were beaten to death inside the camp. During these seven-and-a-half years another estimated 11,060 prisoners were transported to the gas chambers of Bernburg, Auschwitz, and Bergen-Belsen. Not included in these numbers are those who died on work details outside the camp, those who froze or starved on transports to and from the camp, and those who died in transports from the camp that were not officially designated as liquidation transports. In addition to all these, an estimated 7200 Russian prisoners of war were shot through the skull in the camp's stable. The *Report* concludes that "It is therefore certainly still too conservative to set the number of those who died or were murdered under the immediate influence of Buchenwald at 55,000 victims"—roughly the number of Americans who died in Vietnam and only a small fraction of those liquidated in the German camps.

The prisoners were classified into groups, each with a colored triangle sewn on the left shirt front and right pant leg—red for politicals, black for "antisocials," green for criminals, purple for Jehovah's witnesses, pink for homosexuals. Jews wore a yellow triangle underneath their red, black, purple, or pink (there were not only Jewish criminals, homosexuals, and antisocials but also Jewish Jehovah's witnesses), and non-Germans had a letter indicating their nationality printed on their triangles—T for Czech, F for French, etc.

In the morning they were given a half-hour in which to wash and toilet, dress, eat, make their beds, and stand roll call. Then they worked from daybreak till twilight, and sometimes after dark, with a one-hour midday break that included two roll calls. There was a constant shortage of water for washing and drinking, and for some years the only toilets were open latrines which the Jews were assigned to empty.

In the early years most of the daily work involved clearing forests so as to enlarge the camp, establishing and operating an armament factory, and building a road to Weimar. But very soon this work came to include the production of paintings, sculpture, and handcrafted furniture for the SS officers; a 60-foot high equestrian hall for the camp commandant's wife in her morning rides accompanied by a military band; and a personal falconry for Hermann Goering, complete with falconer's residence, aviary, gazebo, and hunting hall with hand carved furniture—none of which Goering ever saw.

In performing this work, artists and skilled craftsmen got preferential treatment, and they were happy to divert from armament production as much labor time and material as possible. For others the easiest work was inside the camp, in the kitchen, laundry, warehouse, or hospital, or in the workshops devoted to tailoring, shoemaking, cabinetry, etc. The camp's prisoner-run infrastructure, staffed increasingly over the years by politicals rather than the criminals and antisocials originally selected by the SS, counseled people on methods of survival, assigned the easier work to invalids, and as much as possible hid Jews from exposure to SS sadism on work details inside and outside the camp. Two everyday forms of this sadism are described as follows:

> The cap of a prisoner would be snatched from his head because it was allegedly dirty. With the words "Go fetch your filthy cap and show it to me clean tomorrow!" the cap would be thrown past the sentries who stood around the work detail. If the prisoner

innocently ran after it, he was shot down for "attempted escape." (33)

The stone quarry was the truest of the 'suicide' work details where several thousand comrades met their deaths through blows from stones...deliberate pushes over the precipice, shooting, and every other type of torment.

A favorite practice of the sergeants was to have candidates for death, especially Jews, push an empty or even loaded cart up a steep slope—an impossible task for one man or two prisoners together. They would be killed by the weight of the cart as it rolled back on them or by the beatings that accompanied the task (51).

These are not Buchenwald's worst atrocities but just the everyday circumstances in which prisoners learned to dissociate their minds from their bodies. "Many could protect their inner worth only by simultaneously entering a state of split consciousness, whereby the body was wholly turned over to the arbitrary outside power while the true self absented itself from the body, observing it psychologically and objectively" (47).

The prisoners' organized infrastructure was instrumental to helping them protect this inner worth—and sometimes their lives—and *The Buchenwald Report* gives many indications that the political prisoners were crucial to operating this infrastructure. On April 11, when the camp was first discovered by two US Army intelligence officers, they reported the following:

[We] turned a corner onto a main highway, and saw thousands of ragged, hungry-looking men, marching in orderly formations.... These men were armed and had leaders at their sides. Some platoons carried German rifles. Some platoons had panzerfausts on their shoulders. Some carried "potato masher" hand grenades. They laughed and waved wildly as they walked...These were the inmates of Buchenwald, walking out to war as tanks swept by at 25 miles an hour."(5)

This was the camp militia organized years earlier by the prisoners, and the US officers' preliminary report included "a short history of the camp and an analysis of camp organization, particularly stressing the role of the Communist-dominated inmate leadership. The officers could not help being impressed that 'instead of a heap of corpses, or a disorderly mob of starving, leaderless men, the Americans found a disciplined and efficient organization in Buchenwald.'"(5)

3.

While Paul and I settled into our daily needle routine, many of our guys found themselves with time on their hands and settled into pillage. One took completely apart a German motorcycle he'd laid claim to, packed it in crates he'd constructed, and sent it home to await him. Three others spent a week diagramming and then disassembling the gorgeous cut glass chandelier in the manor's great entrance hall. They wrapped individually 1200 pieces of glass and crated them to send home, where they were to split the American profits of this European treasure.

Meanwhile, our notorious Captain Mack, the 84th's alcoholic dentist, followed his m.o. of commandeering a jeep and conducting a house-to-house search for miles around to confiscate any liquor he could find to share with his fellow officers. But as it happened, the 84th had a new commanding officer, who, when he saw Mack drive up the great driveway and unload his loot on the manor house steps, ordered loudly before everyone present that the liquor be divided equally among officers and enlisted men. This was our one experience of American democracy in the 84th, and our first drink of anything besides tepid 3.2 beer since we'd left England. That night we passed the bottles round until they were empty and we were smashed, at which point I was sitting on the lap of our truck driver Tommy Thompson, a loudmouth full of casual anti-semitism, and at 2 a.m. more or less apologizing for being a Jew.

I also looked for something to send home, although I didn't covet motorcycles and didn't have much time to root around. But in the basement of what had been the servants' quarters, one of two identical large buildings set at right angles to the manor house at both ends, I found a dozen crates of uniform size and pried one open. On top were several layers of Hitler Youth uniforms, in sizes fitting six- to twelve-year-olds, and underneath them layers of orchestral part scores for the symphonies of Mozart, Beethoven, and Schubert, evidently dating back to a court orchestra. Amongst these was a beautifully bound volume with an engraved score of *Die Zauberflote*, and this became my piece of loot. Of course, being even then "The Bear" that Robin later nicknamed me on Day One of our marriage, the first time I opened this book at home I spilled coffee on the title page.

Our main recreation besides pillage and volleyball was walking on Sundays in the manor's enormous park, complete with a creek and a beer garden, amidst dozens of local families strolling with their children. We mostly ignored them, in accordance with the army's Non-Fraternization Policy, until it gradually came home to us that they had been as astonished as we were by the existence of the concentration camp. At first I didn't believe this—none of us did—and held these Germans all the more in contempt for what seemed the brazen lying beneath their family-value facade. But the army had taken them systematically by cohorts to see the camp, and by now it was inconceivable that they could each and every one have simulated such shock.

The ruins of Aachen, the ghastly crematorium, Hitler Youth layered over Mozart and Beethoven, respectable families shocked to learn the living horror next door—this convergence was beyond explaining in Phil Epstein's communist terms, but it was also beyond comprehension in any political, moral, or religious terms that I had ever heard of. I tried to put it all together, of course couldn't do it, but also couldn't let go, and here is perhaps the subterranean story of my adult life. For it's not as if then or later I made it my agenda to understand what I'd experienced during those three weeks at Buchenwald. But the experience proved indelible; it hasn't faded after 60 years, and for someone who by temperament and chance became an intellectual for most of those years, it has remained an unshakeable point of reference in my professional, political, and personal life.

Life itself may be a mystery, but there is even so a logic to the ways in which we enlarge or destroy our humanity day by day, and untangling this logic is the time-honored vocation of poets and novelists, historians and political economists, in their common concern for the interplay of human suffering and human fulfillment. Perhaps I might have found my way to this vocation without the experience of Buchenwald. But it feels to me now as if that experience gave me little choice while also keeping my choice buried for a long time beneath my conscious awareness.

Like thousands of veterans of America's serial wars, I wouldn't talk for years about the experiences that affected me, and it's only in the last decade that I've been comfortable telling people I was at Buchenwald whenever it seemed relevant—which it did in February, 2003 at the Jose Marti airport in Havana when our tour group was breaking up to go home. We were having a last political discussion while sitting on our luggage at the check-in line, and I was the one holdout for whom our Cuban experience, among its many pleasures, had also been politically inspiring. In trying to explain myself concerning Cuba, which I will also try to do later in this book, I talked about Buchenwald, and of how what we'd seen of the Cuban people's struggle hinted at an attainable human future in which anything like Buchenwald—or Dresden, Hiroshima, My Lai, or Fallujah—would have become contrary to human nature. A journalist in our group, Inda Schaenen, then told how two of her uncles had also seen concentration camps, and how the experience had unstrung them for the rest of their lives. No matter how hurt or calloused the war might have made you, this wasn't something you could just weather and let fade, and in that respect we liberators might have been worse off than the camps' actual survivors. Many of them I've heard about are joyous, un-preoccupied people, evidently so grateful for life that their trauma was not repressed but simply purged from consciousness.

Thinking about Inda's uncles also made me think how my politicization by Buchenwald has affected my capacity for life ever since. Not that I've had a dull life, but that its everyday horizon has been more limited than I might have liked. I don't have wide interests or very much small talk. I don't read just for the love of reading, even if within my horizon I may read more than those who do. I've always been relieved to tag along with my wives in pursuing their interests in hiking or cooking or women's sports, since I've had few interests of my own beyond politics and music, which are too intense to share easily. As if all this weren't enough, I inherited from my dear mother, along with many qualities for which I am grateful beyond words, a temperamental disposition to be critical, which was of course deepened by my professional training. Nothing could feed better my sour disposition than the history of my beloved country during my lifetime. Reading a newspaper or novel, watching a movie or sports event, the first thing I notice is what's wrong—the ideological slant of the news, the consumerist commodification of sport, the movie's political evasions—and, like many academics, I can't wait to expound my critique to anyone who will listen. Long ago my dear Robin, who begins by welcoming the world as it is and only then may open it to critique, learned to shut me off before I get started—and to leave me out on a limb chewing my sour cud.

4.

We did what we could at Buchenwald. Some of our sick died, others recovered and went home, and my sub-unit of the 84th was sent on to establish a hospital for newly liberated prisoners of war in Gera, a city about to become part of communist East Germany. Here we were joined by eighteen Russian medics who had been war prisoners, by a cohort of German nurses from Gera itself, and by a multilingual French dentist, also a released prisoner, who could translate our English into German for the nurses and Russians, and their German into English for us. Our patients were Poles, French, Croats, Dutch, Hungarians, and Czechs, all locked like us inside their native languages. Together we made an embryonic United Nations inside a vibrating Tower of Babel.

I remember Gera as a grimy red brick city right out of Dickens. The army had commandeered a school building for our hospital, along with the apartment house across the street, whose tenants had been temporarily relocated so that we and the Russians could live in their quarters complete with furniture and utensils. The German nurses had been long taught to hate Russians, and they now had every reason to hate us for killing their men, destroying their cities, and living in their neighbors' apartments. But healing was their profession, and among the first things they did—in concert with the Russians!—was to scour the neighborhood trees, shrubs, and flowers for anything they could harmlessly cut to decorate our schoolroom bed wards. They also found sketch-pads, crayons, and decks of cards for the patients, and they brought in a harmonica for our musical one-armed Croatian. But as far as I remember, not one of those nurses ever cracked a smile. The joyous Russians tried to loosen them up, some of us Americans tried gently to tease them, but they remained strictly business.

Our patients were all malnourished, although nothing like the Buchenwald survivors, and our mess sergeant was at his best in cooking to restore their vitality. Some had fevers, some cracked bones, some open wounds, some big cysts, and almost everyone rotting teeth. Our procedure for diagnosis and treatment was a howl. The Russian M.D. accompanied by his orderly with notebook and pencil, our Captain Evans accompanied by me with notebook and pencil, and the French dentist made rounds together. When we five came to a Polish patient, one of the Russians would ask him about his condition in some kind of pidgin Slavic, translate his answer into German for the French dentist, who then translated it into English for us. Or Captain Evans would examine a Dutchman and tell his findings to the Russian M.D. by way of the French dentist. Then the two doctors consulted via the dentist, and decided not only on a diagnosis and treatment but also on who should administer it, them or us. If it was us, I wrote it up in my notebook; if the Russians, their orderly in his notebook; and as it turned out, our two medical heads were better than one. Captain Evans observed regularly how the Russian saw things that he didn't, and he clearly knew plenty that the Russian didn't.

Meanwhile, we became short of expendables: needles and syringes, anesthetic and sulfa drugs, gauze, tape, plaster. But our nurses managed to find some locally produced *ersatz*: flimsy plastic syringes, paper gauze and plaster bandage. I was our dedicated cast man, and for our patients with cracked bones I produced decently durable casts out of paper bandage and multiple thin layers of plaster. Surgery was not in order here, but on occasion we cut out cysts from shoulders, legs, or armpits by anesthetizing the affected area with skin-deep ethyl chloride, which was all we had, and then two of us fiercely holding the patient down while Captain Evans proceeded with his scalpel.

There was no loot to be had in Gera, but there were girls. The Non-Fraternization Policy was ignored after dark, and mornings when I came in from night shift, my apartment mates would be rolling out of bed with their partners. A couple of these women conveyed by signs their admiration for my straight white teeth and their regret they hadn't known about me sooner. But I was dead tired, they were already taken, and nothing ever came of it. I'd have a beer with my faithfully married buddy, Corporal Robert Haff—his wake-up and my nightcap—and fall into bed. Then in the afternoon I'd write letters home about our international community, especially the Russians.

They were more innocently light-hearted than our guys, more frank and joyous, which of course could have come from their being just released prisoners. But I imagined it was also a matter of national character, and when decades later I read Dostoevsky, there was no way I could square his tormented Russians with those I had worked with in Gera, who were more like Tolstoy's peasant soldiers. They drank anything alcoholic that came to hand, and there was even a rumor that on their way to this assignment some of them died from imbibing aircraft fuel. But they also sang and danced, played innocent pranks, and showed sober affection for their patients and each other—nothing like Raskolnikov or Stavrogin, nor like your stereotyped Stakhanovite heroically surpassing his production quota. For the weeks we were together, those Russians made our hospital a fun place to be even amidst its surroundings and operations.

In its grim way Gera was a relief from Buchenwald, maybe even a teasing hint of possible renewal after the barbarism. War prisoners liberated, Americans, Germans, and Russians working harmoniously together, patients from all countries recovering jointly before going home separately—an international healing of body and spirit. At moments all this felt to me like an alternative to war: left to our own devices in the work of healing, we had overcome among ourselves the divisions and suspicions on which war feeds. But then of course came the question of whether, how, or when people like us would ever be empowered to use our own devices. Our patients were returning to their helpless homelands, the people of Gera were about to become part of the East German nightmare, and we Americans were about to add our Pacific postscript to the European Holocaust at Hiroshima and Nagasaki.

Gera was our last assignment in Europe before being reassigned to the Pacific and sent to Marseilles, and that story can be told quickly. Outside Gera we were loaded onto freight cars— the famous 40 & 8s (capacity 40 humans or 8 horses) that had carried hundreds of thousands to the concentration camps. We each had a canvas cot, and the train stopped each day for lunch and supper while the cooks made our meals at trackside and we improvised latrines behind them. We ran day and night for a week, finally arriving at a huge staging area just east of Marseilles where tens of thousands of American troops were awaiting ships. Those units with the most "points"—for total length of service, length of overseas service, number of individual battle stars—were on their way home to be discharged. The rest, including the 84th with its skimpy six months in Europe and only one battle star, were being sent through the Panama Canal to join the island-hopping war against Japan.

We spent six stupefying weeks outside Marseilles, and up to the day we boarded a ship, I remember only scattered details. One is that I had sex for the first time. A Frenchman brought his wife to the 84th's tent compound, and in the dead of night we lined up by dozens to enjoy her—three minutes for $1 to the cashier husband (or $2 for half-and-half)—and then be shooed away quickly to make way for the next in line. I might have gone on to livelier adventures of this kind if my luck hadn't turned. Four times during those six weeks we drew lots to see who'd win three-day passes to Paris, and I was a winner the first three times. But all three times the passes were cancelled because a ship was supposedly ready for us, which it wasn't, which is just like the Army. The fourth time I lost, and the winners went to Paris.

We swam sometimes at a beach near the camp whose shallow water was swarming with jellyfish, and we did get passes to go in to Marseilles, whose harbor was dotted by half-sunken ships sticking up at crazy angles, and whose streets were eerily empty, as if the entire city in its gorgeous sunlight had shuttered itself against us GI hordes. Bars were open here and there where you could get a grudging beer, but I don't remember actually seeing any people outdoors. Our exit from Europe was a chilling good riddance six months after our wild welcome at Liege.

In the early dawn of August 7, 1945, as we stood in line to board the ship that would carry us through the Panama Canal, the dock was full of Red Cross volunteers serving donuts and coffee, along with copies of the army newspaper, *Stars and Stripes*. The headline story announced the bombing of Hiroshima the day before, and with it a scale of death that was new to humanity's capacity for self-destruction. We were stunned, but our first reaction of pity for the victims passed quickly into the consuming hope that we could now be spared the Pacific. And where Buchenwald was an immediate experience in the direct line of duty, Hiroshima's remoteness and scale of instant destruction have made it for me a kind of abstraction then and ever since. Or maybe it's that once you try coming to terms with Buchenwald, Hiroshima isn't all that different.

For three days while our ship headed toward Panama, all we talked about was the possibility the war would end now and we could avoid the grisly Pacific. The army rumor mill ran double overtime, and then on our fourth day out, while the 84th was taking its afternoon turn on deck to imbibe fresh air, a big deep voice came booming over the ship's loudspeaker: "NOW HEAR THIS! This is the captain speaking. Look to the stern and follow the wake of the ship as we turn toward New York."

All hell broke loose, and I've somehow imagined all this time that in jumping up and down while hugging strangers by the dozens, we actually rocked the boat. People yelled, wept, prayed, danced, in a mass surge of energy such as I have never experienced since, even at a Washington civil rights demonstration of 100,000 people. We were not going to die in this war, and the repressed fear that soldiers live with all the time could begin to dissolve. The Hiroshima bomb was our good luck.

It was also for me a second stroke of luck that probably saved my life. When I entered the army in 1943, I went through basic training at the famous Fort Benning Infantry School, where I became an accomplished infantry marksman. Then I was among those who scored well enough on a test to be selected for the Army Specialized Training Program, an intensive, college-level program designed to produce in just six months German and Japanese translators, cryptographers, para-engineers, and military government personnel whom the Army anticipated it would need before the war was over. My group was sent to study engineering at Purdue University, where I weirdly managed to get A's on the first couple of quizzes in calculus and physics. Then after six weeks, and before my underlying ineptitude for science could be exposed, the program was shut down, the Army having decided it had enough engineers. We were reassigned to an infantry unit being assembled at Camp Swift, Texas and given a weekend pass before being shipped out. On that weekend in Chicago I got pneumonia, had to be hospitalized for a month, and was left behind when my buddies went to Texas. While I languished in bed with visits from my parents, they were formed into the commando unit that later became world famous as "Roger's Rangers"—the first Americans to cross the Rhine, and in so doing to be all but wiped out. I learned later that my best friend among them, Richard Golbus, with whom I'd double-dated with his fiancée and her girlfriend the night I got pneumonia, was shot dead crossing the river, age 20.

An accident of illness had saved me from death as a commando, the date of Hiroshima had me going home safely for good, and who knows how many thousands of American soldiers owe their lives in this way to the blind goddess Fortune? For some of these, the sheer luck of survival induces sheer recklessness once they get home. For others like Robin's father, it induces a single-minded pursuit of financial and emotional security. And for others like me it induces a search for purpose to validate a life that's been randomly spared. My war experience was leading me, inexorably if still unknowingly, to look for that purpose in the pursuit of social justice no matter where life might lead me.

CHAPTER 2. WINDOWS OF OPPORTUNITY:

CHICAGO, 1946-1949

I have very little memory of my reunion with my family after we docked in New York. Not only did the 84th lack enough points for immediate discharge, but our medical specialties were still in demand at the army hospitals in this country ministering to thousands of American wounded who needed long-term treatment and healing. We were given a week's leave to go home, and there I realized, really for the first time, how much my parents had worried that their chubby son might not make it. Their deep relief was evident beneath their joy at seeing me, and I regaled them with stories of swimming through the jellyfish and our mid-Atlantic turn-around. Just like when I was a kid, I went downtown on the "L" to have lunch with my dad and his lawyer cronies, only now showing off in my staff sergeant's dress uniform. I went shopping with my mom at Marshall Field's, I took my sister Mimi, now a high school sophomore, to the American Ballet Theater, and after dinner we four would go to the drug store for 5c ice cream cones just like always. My brother Chuck was away in college at DePauw, and I didn't get to see him until I was discharged six months later and Chuck trounced our dad and me, game after game all afternoon, at the neighborhood pool hall.

The 84th spent its last six months at Nichols General Hospital in Louisville. Although called general hospitals, these installations typically specialized in two or more interrelated diagnostics and treatments. At Nichols it was bone and nerve grafting, sometimes brain surgery, occasionally amputation. Our typical patient would be missing a section of bone and nerve in a shattered arm or leg, or else a kneecap. On Mondays, Wednesdays, and Fridays we replaced the missing bone segments or kneecaps, and on Tuesdays and Thursdays we re-attached the severed nerves. A typical bone procedure would be to take a slice of tibia from the leg, using a circular saw with parallel blades whose distance from each other and depth of cut could be adjusted as necessary. Then while one surgeon sewed up the donor tibia, which would regenerate over time, the other screwed the removed slice of bone across the gap in a humerus or femur. Weeks later, after this graft had taken, we opened the limb again, straightened or bent the joint as required to produce slack in the nerve, and sewed together the severed nerve ends. We then stabilized the joint with a cast, and a couple of weeks later replaced this cast with another that bent the joint at a small angle. Then at intervals we shrank or enlarged this angle in order to stretch the nerve gradually until, 95% of the time, the arm or leg was functional again.

On Mondays, Wednesdays, and Fridays our operating room looked like a carpenter's shop with its array of saws, drills, screwdrivers, mallets, and chisels. On Tuesdays and Thursdays it looked like a tailor's shop with its array of threads, needles, tweezers, and forceps. And every day it looked like a butcher shop with its ooze of blood and body fluids. There were five operating rooms, as I remember, and we began at 7.30 in the morning, with three to five surgeries a day scheduled for each room. If they all went smoothly, we could get a morning coffee break, a lunch break, and still be done by 3 or 4 in the afternoon. That would be a boon to us technicians who had to clear away the mess, wash everything down with killer chemicals, and then run the autoclaves and package the instrument sets for the next day's surgeries. Then on alternate evenings after supper, we went off to the wards to shave the arms, legs, or skulls of those scheduled for tomorrow's saws and scalpels. I hated shaving skulls, which I invariably nicked with my naked razor blade, but I loved making casts.

At first I felt a kind of vocational excitement at learning to do a lot of new things properly, and often under pressure. At these stateside hospitals, the scrub nurses—those who hand the surgeons the instruments inside the sterile field—were women RN army lieutenants. Paul and I had also been trained to scrub, but our job here was to be "circulating technicians," moving in and out of the sterile field to remove bloodied swabs and linens, used instruments, or pans of bone chips, and to hand the scrub nurses fresh instruments, containers, or supplies without compromising the sterile field.

We were also responsible for safety when the electric saws were in use. At intervals while cutting out the tibia slice, the surgeons had to put down the saw on the patient's stomach, and they risked stepping on the foot pedal accidentally while checking their progress before resuming cutting. They were required to say "OFF" when they put the saw down, at which point we had to stop whatever we were doing, remove the electric plug from a wall socket outside the sterile field, and repeat "OFF." When they were ready to resume they were required to say "ON," and we reinserted the plug and repeated "ON." But surgeons being surgeons in their intense absorption, some ignored this requirement and expected us to anticipate them, which we couldn't always do. So a couple of times I risked their wrath by refusing to plug in until they said "On" and then yelling "OFF" when they put the saw down. They got the message and I got some credit.

I also refined my skill at making plaster casts suited to all occasions and conditions, and I became the preferred circulating technician working with the preferred scrub nurse of our chief brain surgeon, whose delicacy of touch was accompanied by a very short temper. If the slightest detail went just slightly awry, he was as likely as not to throw a tray of instruments on the floor while cursing us all, and you couldn't let yourself be rattled while cleaning up the mess and producing a new tray immediately. From what I could see, this man salvaged a couple dozen lives.

But as my expertise and sense of accomplishment grew during six months of three to five surgeries a day (among perhaps 2000 performed during that time in this one hospital), so did my awareness of the human trauma and suffering produced by war on a terrible scale among those who survive. Buchenwald and Hiroshima were (we still hope) one-time events that dwarf the imagination, and now that we were home Germany and Japan seemed comfortably remote. But thousands of American boys whose bodies were sawed, screwed, and sewn back together at Nichols, or fitted with artificial limbs, paraplegic bags, or complicated whatnots at other hospitals, now had to return to their families and communities with a Sears Catalogue variety of shrunken lifestyles and shortened life-expectancies. One of my high school classmates came home in a wheelchair, one with a missing leg, others minus an eye or a testicle, and then there were those with skin grafts.

A hospital in Memphis specialized in skin grafting, and we regularly had to take patients whose bone and nerve repairs were healed on an overnight train to Memphis, where their restored arms, legs, knees, and skulls would receive a new outer layer. My first shock on entering that Memphis hospital made me almost forget Buchenwald, and I can still call up this image any hour of the day or night: dozens of otherwise healthy men walking the corridors with their rebuilt faces—eye sockets, jaws, noses, ears— all newly sheathed in grafted skin whose color ran from purple to ochre to mustard within the vaguely restored contours of a face this twenty-something now had to turn toward the world for the rest of a lifetime.

Those trips to Memphis got me thinking about pacifism. Phil, Paul, and I had talked a lot about the difference between just and unjust wars, and, like most Americans back then, we thought the war we were fighting was just. Since that war against Hitler's Germany, the question of just war has been subject to learned debate all across the political spectrum in connection with America's open-ended series of subsequent wars. But the question now seems to me so theoretically abstract, just like the question of violent revolution, as to mask its human meaning. The Leninist argument that a capitalist class feeling threatened will always be the one to initiate violence has proved no less valid than the argument that if you give Hitler an inch he will take an ell. But wars and revolutions that conceivably can be justified in theory turn out in practice to produce Hiroshima, the Gulag, and Abu Ghraib, and over the decades since I saw that hospital in Memphis, I've wondered more than once whether even our war prevented more death and suffering than it produced.

Over those decades America has developed a cultural addiction to war that keeps killing millions of people for no lasting purpose, and in that process disables our minds and empties our souls. On flimsy pretexts we demonize enemies in Korea, Vietnam, Iraq, or Iran (to name only those), and our most lasting accomplishment in defeating these enemies appears to be no more than the body count of the dead. Our media publish daily tallies of this accomplishment, and when the next demon is named we're ready for a new fix. Each time we are told that a war must be fought in order to maintain peace, yet peace remains somehow always out of reach The pacifist A.J. Muste said, "There is no way to peace. Peace is the way," and the army colonel Hugo Chavez introduced socialism to Venezuela by renouncing violence and offering redundant re-election in response to CIA violence. What I sensed inchoately in that Memphis hospital found a voice decades later when I saw the bumper sticker message, "War Is Not The Answer."

So it was that that when we were about to be discharged from the army after six months at Nichols, I turned down two tempting offers of a whole adult life. The 84th's Captain Evans offered to pay my way through medical school, and the US Army offered Paul Leder and me promotion to master sergeant, the highest enlisted rank, plus a choice of any operating room in the world—Paris (finally!), Tokyo, Walter Reed in Washington, D.C—if we would re-enlist for a 20- or 30-year hitch. I was so flattered by Captain Evans' offer that it almost turned my head. But while our bio-medical training as technicians had been engaging intellectually, it hadn't inspired me vocationally. I was even more tempted by the Army's offer to see the world while continuing to help people heal, then retire on a master sergeant's pension at 40 or 50 and choose a career sequel that might appeal to my maturity. But by now I had sensed that my skill at making plaster casts and enduring surgeons' tantrums didn't add up to even a 20-year calling, and the salary, perks, and retirement prospects of a master sergeant, awesome as they seemed then, could not erase what I had seen in those Louisville and Memphis hospitals. I declined both offers, which brought me a step closer to the vocation I found.

2.

On alternate nights members of the surgical staff were on call and had to stay on the hospital grounds. So those were good nights for writing letters, and the place Paul and I found to write them was the hospital's music room, soundproofed and stocked by the citizens of Louisville with a wide collection of popular and classical albums (78 rpm). Only two or three times during our six months did I see in this room any of the patients for whom it was intended. But it became a hangout for us, and also the short-tempered brain surgeon, who would smoke his pipe, allow us to choose the music, and seldom say a word. Here began my immersion of mind, emotion, and spirit in Western classical music.

My father's family were musically gifted. His father had been a synagogue cantor, he and his brother Ben had fine tenor voices, and their sister Sylvia was a talented self-taught pianist. While selling shoes to put himself through law school, my dad was an usher at Chicago's Lyric Opera House, and many Friday evenings we greeted the Sabbath with all the aunts, uncles, and cousins gathered round Sylvia's piano singing Gershwin, Cole Porter, or Irving Berlin, with an occasional aria by Verdi or Puccini. Chuck and I took violin lessons until they began interfering with sports, I sang in my high school chorus, and after graduating Harvard Law School Chuck became an admired folk guitarist. So I was ripe for exposure to classical music, and, as with so many initiates, my first loves were strongly melodic and lavishly orchestrated works by Mendelssohn, Tchaikovsky, and Rimsky-Korsakov. I also learned then how the glories of Mozart, Beethoven, and Berlioz can be discovered only by repeated listening, and I've been listening ever since.

On the alternate nights when we were free to leave the hospital, Paul and I made the rounds of Louisville bars and restaurants. We were both drinkers, and we soon settled on a bar whose martinis and Shrimp Arnaud were exceptional. Then we'd move on to a boilerplate restaurant for dinner—Chinese, Italian, Steakhouse, or the original Colonel Sanders', where we were greeted once by a white suited, white-haired elderly person who I believe was the man himself.

In those restaurants and bars we rehashed the day's surgical soap opera and then talked a lot about literature and politics. Paul was a Broadway actor whose striking looks and sexy voice reminded everyone of the movie star Cary Grant (including, once, Cary Grant). He was a great raconteur and had a single enrapturing literary interest—the novels of Thomas Wolfe. He and his high school girlfriend were steeped in Wolfe's writing and had made a hitchhiking pilgrimage to Wolfe's native place, Asheville, NC, which had become a tourist destination. But I can't believe Wolfe ever had a histrio like Paul Leder who could make his blousy rhetoric sound plausible. Almost anything we talked about could remind Paul of a passage in Wolfe, and off he'd go. I thought his renditions more moving than Wolfe's writing, and when twenty years later I became a colleague of William Charvat, who'd been Wolfe's office mate at NYU, Charvat's account of Wolfe's drunken flights brought back to my ears Paul's great riffs in those Louisville bars.

But our most nourishing experience of rest and recovery from the daily operating room grind—and also our now wearying years of army life—was the weekends we spent with the Kort family. My mother had suggested we look up her childhood friend Florence Kort, a plump, stately, prematurely gray woman who wore a pince-nez and in whose magical aura we soon came to bask. She and her husband Herman had a daughter away in college, and two teenage daughters and a four-year-old son at home. We were enough older than Loyce and Doris (always called "Putch")—and further exalted by our army uniforms—to put romantic interest out of the question, and this was part of our ease in that household. It was like family. Paul and I were good dancers, and we spent hours dancing on the sun porch—Paul and Loyce jitterbugging wildly or going at the Charleston, Putch and I sedately essaying the waltz or the two-step. I in fact taught Putch to dance, and we soon developed a fine-tuned ease of rhythm and flow, trusting each other until we produced a levitating unity of motion that I have not experienced since.

Putch was very much her mother's daughter, and I remember Florence Kort as magnificent. She had my mother's sharpness and curiosity about the world, plus a rare generosity of outlook. She worried aloud that Paul and I over that length of time were spoiling her daughters for boys their own age, but she also said we were bringing a richness into their lives that they would not regret. She was interested in my politics, I was interested in her shrewd observations of people and events, and she secretly wrote my mother her worry about my drinking. My deepest memory is of Sunday mornings after breakfast, when the two of us sat knee to knee facing each other with a pan on the floor between us, peeling potatoes, carrots, and whatnot for whatever she might be roasting for dinner, and talking non-stop for a couple of hours about everything. Then at dinner Herman would produce his black market Madeira, and this always seemed to me like just the right wine for any meal Florence might have prepared.

3.

What with Florence Kort's Sunday dinners, our Louisville restauranting, and our mid-morning snacks between surgeries at the hospital, I weighed 205 pounds at 5'11" when I was discharged from the army at Fort Sheridan, Illinois on 31March1946, some three months before my 21st birthday. When I got home late that afternoon, my 5'4" wisp of a mother Fritzie greeted me with a bottle of bourbon, and then after dinner drank me under the table while listening to my stories. I've gone on drinking for the rest of my life, but thanks to Florence Kort and my mom back then, I've known my limits most of the time.

My father Alex was now three inches shorter and forty pounds lighter than I was, and he'd only read in the newspapers what I had seen first-hand. Almost from the time we could walk, he had pushed us kids to adventure on life in the city. At age five, I believe, Chuck was taking two streetcars to his violin lessons (2c half-fare carrying a quarter-size violin), and often on Saturdays we two took the bus to Lincoln Park or the Field Museum, where we linked up with our cousins Marvin and Howard Wolfberg. Now my dad deferred effortlessly to me on many family matters. That first week home he gave me money to buy us an up-to-date phonograph (Webcor Portable) and a couple of classical albums to get started on—with a warning they shouldn't be too classical. I came home with Brahms's Fourth Symphony and Tchaikovsky's Romeo and Juliet, and to both our relief he liked them both well.

During all the time I can remember, both before the war and after, my father came home from the office dead tired. I'd often get him his slippers when he walked in the door, and he spent many whole evenings after dinner lying on the couch. The music I brought home that spring and summer refreshed him, but now it also occurred to me to wonder, as I had never done before, why he was so regularly worn out.

At family gatherings and picnics he was always the life of the party. He told Jewish jokes with a finely honed Yiddish accent and an exquisite sense of timing. He was also a big practical joker, and he sprinkled affectionate nicknames among his in-laws and friends. He'd be the one to get the softball game going at a picnic, or the singing, and after supper the gin rummy among the uncles at a penny a point. He organized the Thursday afternoon bowling for his lawyer network, and he exchanged mocking letters with out-of-town relatives. When Chuck and I were kids he took us to Wrigley Field, taught us to swing the bat and swim in Lake Michigan, and when I became an awkward adolescent who was chosen next-to-last for pick-up softball or football, he got me doing drills and running around the block until I was picked second or third.

Yet his life had another side, which I came to comprehend only after he died that autumn of a cerebral hemorrhage at age 48. There was nothing secret or obscure about it; it had always been right there, only I hadn't put it together. As my mother then wondered and I now believe, he was mentally and emotionally worn out by the Depression, and this fed into his cardiovascular inheritance. His father died young of a stroke, and he was a pack-a-day smoker. But over and beyond that he was a caring person who never talked the talk but always walked the walk, and for a Depression adult who was this outgoing and had this big a network of family and friends, his caring exacted a big toll.

He struggled first of all to succeed as a lawyer and make his own family secure. On school holidays in my boyhood when I came downtown to have lunch with him, a big adventure for me, I'd often find him practicing at writing his signature with an elegant flourish. A story his friends loved to tell was how after graduating law school he kept making excuses for not joining them to usher at the opera. When they finally confronted him, he said this would look undignified and scare off prospective clients. (One of these was a Chicago newspaper columnist whose headline the next morning was "The Fall of the House of Usher"). Yet despite his Dreiser-ian pretensions, almost the only cases my father got in his early years were referred to him by a colleague and involved foreclosing home mortgages on people unable to keep up their monthly payments. This only made him feel guilty, and he worked hard to get free of it. But then in his last years when his law practice finally took off, it brought him self-made rich clients who invited him to dinner parties where after the meal a black servant came round to light the gentlemen's cigars. This my dad could not stand, and he found ways to elude these invitations just as he had ushering at the opera.

Between his first years of foreclosing mortgages and his last years of handsome fees from people who made him socially uncomfortable (one of his friends told us that if he'd lived a few years longer he'd have become a millionaire), my father was constantly involved in schemes to keep his relatives and friends on their feet. He was the only member of his family to become a college-educated professional, and it seems never to have occurred to him not to use his knowledge and money to help everyone near and dear to him. Early in the Depression his brother Ben was barely making a living selling auto parts, and also his sister Rose's husband Bernie as an electrician. These two went in together on a window-shade business, and my dad helped with the start-up money and legal work. A few years later he and Uncle Bernie established the Midwest Cabinet and Stand Co., which produced replacement cabinets for tavern jukeboxes and of which I was the sole employee. They rented a downtown warehouse room where I came after school and, after being instructed by my uncle, wired up dozens of prefabricated cabinets to produce their moving light displays. This business lasted just more than a year and I believe lost money.

He sometimes helped out two of his cousins who had a shoe store where the entire family bought our shoes. He paid the rent and brought home the weekly laundry of a bachelor uncle who was blind and sat all day on a wooden chair with his hands in his lap.. He helped support my mother's sister Irene the artist, he fell for a scam by a Jewish jailbird to help get him a parole, and he was a major contributor to bringing two families of distant relatives out of Germany. A cellist friend, Max Green, was struggling with a ladies' dress shop, and my dad went to their circle of friends and produced enough capital to start a second shop and eventual success story—after the war Max opened a third shop on Michigan Avenue's Magnificent Mile and sent his two children to college. Another friend, Charlie Jeffe, had failed in the drapery business before my father raised money to set him up with a small grocery store. This also failed, and Charlie promptly died, leaving a widow and two teenage daughters in a bungalow.

His turning-point venture was the Commodore Hotel, an aging 100-room establishment he bought in partnership with his great lawyer friend Julius Polikoff. Something like seventy rooms had permanent occupants—salesmen, secretaries, cashiers, and a hard-drinking *Herald-American* sports columnist, Wayne Otto, who affected to mentor me as sports editor of my high school paper and swing shift bellhop at the hotel. Another block of rooms was regularly occupied by musicians in that era's big bands— Woody Herman's, Glenn Miller's, Artie Shaw's—who played Chicago's fabled lakefront hotel, the Edgewater Beach, just a few blocks away. The remaining rooms were the margin of profit, and they were mostly the scenes of one-night stands.

More weekends than not over five or six years, my father spent hours at the hotel hiring clerks, attending to maintenance, arranging to carry over permanent residents who fell behind in their rent. He nursed the place into making a little money, and then discovered just before I came home that his once dependable manager and wife had taken up embezzling. That was also the year his sister Sylvia's teenage son was killed in an auto accident, and now, six months after my return, while weeping over Billy's grave beside his brother Ben, my dad collapsed, and by the time Ben got him home he was gone.

So here's my (marxian) understanding of my father's life as a contradiction that was sustained only at a withering expense of spirit. His sense of embededness among family and friends, of being all in the Depression together, made him a practical socialist. His ambition to have a memorable signature, $10,000 a year, and a freestanding house with yard, dog, and kids going off to college, made him an awkward bourgeois. (During the war my parents in fact bought a dog, a pit bull they named "Timoshenko" after the Soviet general who drove Hitler's army from Moscow, and then had to give away because he terrorized all the dogs in the neighborhood.) Meanwhile, this Alex Markels couldn't help but sing, tell stories, and play softball when not lying on the couch all worn down by the pressures of his life. His favorite literary quotation was from Shakespeare, the closing lines of Mark Antony's funeral oration for Julius Caesar:

His life was gentle, and the elements

So mix'd in him that Nature might stand up
And say to all the world, "This was a man!"
4.

My father's understanding of his life and times made him a Democratic Party stalwart who revered FDR. and belonged to liberal organizations that were to become embattled (or disappear) in the Cold War years following his death. We kids grew up inside this understanding. His and my mother's liberalism was a defining condition of our lives, and my war experience confirmed this liberalism as at very least a political starting point. It also opened my mind to the radicalism represented by Phil Epstein, and now also by any number of people I met in America's postwar political ferment.

Soon after I got home I applied to return to the University of Wisconsin, where I'd gone for a school year and a summer session before the army, and also to Harvard, which I could now afford because of the GI Bill of Rights. But of course every ex-GI in America was applying to Harvard, and they wrote back a really considerate letter explaining their predicament and urging me to return to Wisconsin. I have never forgiven them. So after working the summer of '46 as a lifeguard on Chicago's beaches, as I had also done the summer of '42, I went back to Madison in September. My father died a few weeks later, and I came home after fall semester to live with my mother and enroll at the University of Chicago.

Now began a period, January 1947 to September 1949— just a little longer than I'd been in the army—of intellectual and political excitement, confusion, and maybe growth. Following my political interests, I sampled at the university a variety of courses in the social sciences—economics and history, sociology, psychology, and anthropology. Then I went halfway through law school, where once in the men's room I peed alongside Robert Maynard Hutchins, before deciding finally to burn my bridges and try for a Ph.D. in English.

Outside the university I became a political activist in The American Veterans Committee. I met Bobby Stone, an aspiring novelist who worked in an office, and during our courtship and first year of marriage we became friends with the communist artist Bernard Goss and familiar acquaintances of Chicago's triumvirate of proletarian writers, Nelson Algren, Jack Conroy, and Willard Motley. I shook hands with W.E.B. DuBois and Paul Robeson at a 1948 rally of Henry Wallace's Progressive Party, and where my intellectual experience at the university led me away from the studies that seemed natural for the politico I was becoming, my activist experience in the city soon led me to join the Communist Party.

My best friend from high school, George Soter, was majoring in sociology, so I sampled that and, in my supercilious arrogance, thought it ephemeral. Another high school classmate, Joe Elbein, was now a fervent marxist majoring in economics and urging me to do the same. So I gave that a try and found it intellectually challenging but not really satisfying even when I managed to rise to the challenge. It felt too abstruse to me, and *Das Kapital, Volume One* was no exception. History, on the other hand, felt far too often mindlessly quotidian. The information could be colorful and intriguing, but I must have been looking even then for a grand narrative, and these were to be found only outside the classroom. I thought Spengler's *The Decline of the West* much more exciting than all those textbook inventories of the causes of the Industrial Revolution or the American Civil War.

I'm not sure I can reconstruct the process through which I then decided to go to law school. My oedipal awe of my father was surely involved, as was my sense that the legal profession would enable me to make a secure living while working for social justice in a step beyond my father—perhaps as a labor or civil liberties lawyer. But I was also thinking that the study of law, besides producing a living, would enable me to extend, deepen, and unify the interests I'd been trying to cultivate. I had a half-formed sense that a nation's law was its constantly evolving, deep structure philosophy of collective life, combining theory and practice in a manner I'd find intellectually interesting and politically purposeful.

I talked it over with my mother, who'd been fascinated by the law for similar reasons in her pre-marital days as a legal stenographer, and she strongly encouraged me. Then as it happened, the University of Chicago Law School conceived its curriculum exactly in the manner of my musings. In those days Chicago and Yale had the reputation of being "philosophical" law schools in contrast to Harvard and Columbia as vocational institutes. Their faculties included philosophers, economists, and anthropologists as well as legal scholars, and at Chicago we were required as freshmen to take a year-long course in the philosophy of law along with the standard introductions to torts, contracts, and negotiable instruments.

This course, "Elements of the Law," was taught by Edward H. Levi, later President Ford's Attorney General, and it was the most exciting intellectual experience I'd had yet. Levi and his Yale colleague Roscoe Pound had put together a three-volume anthology of mimeographed excerpts from the writings of Plato and Aristotle, Locke, Hobbes, Montesquieu, and Rousseau, Adam Smith and Karl Marx, Justices Holmes, Brandeis, Cardozo, and Frankfurter, variously grouped around particular topics. Each volume was around four inches thick, and Levi would often single out particular passages for discussion, so we had to lug the damned book to class. Our reward was some exciting, unpredictable, open-ended exchange between teacher and students, unheard of in my other law classes, where the pedagogical format was question-and-answer but the professors' only questions were "What's the right answer?"

Levi made it exciting by his choice of readings and the questions he posed in relating them to each other and the social problems they addressed. But we also made it exciting by the intensity of our interest and response. As GI Bill students who felt lucky to be here and determined to seize the day, I believe we really were more serious on the whole than the generations I later taught for forty years. Not all of us, of course, and not all of them. Probably a majority of my law school classmates were focused on vocational training and more or less indifferent to the issues Levi was raising. But a whole lot of us were turned on, and Levi was the first of my many teachers in those years who commented outside class how they were being intellectually challenged as never before by us returning GI's.

The vocational courses shared with Levi's course a primary focus on the close reading of texts, either judicial opinions or legislative enactments. The challenge of each night's homework in case law was to figure out the judge's *ratio decidendi*—the single underlying principle or consideration (if there was one) on which his decision actually turned, and the way in which this *ratio* extended, limited, or modified the application of previous judges' decisions on this subject. The challenge with legislation was to figure out the legislators' intent, and in both cases we had to sort out the ambiguities, digressions, and redundancies of individual texts—just as you would have to do in reading *Paradise Lost* or listening to the late sonatas of Schubert.

This study of a text's internal structure, (dis)unity, and (in)coherence engaged me intellectually as nothing else had done. For one thing, it spoke to my efforts in writing sports for my high school paper, letters home from the army, and short stories for the creative writing course I'd taken at Wisconsin. But far more important than that, it showed me as never before the connection between our construction of discourse and our experience of the world. Not that I could have said it this way then. But what had begun for me as sporadic glimmers of a society's collective unconscious expressed in the language of its law now became a general awareness of deliberated discourse as both a reflection and a construction of human reality.

My enlargement of vision was also accelerated by my weekly lunchtime discussions with a group of law school classmates and graduate students in English. I don't remember now how the two got connected, but it was at a seedy Irish pub under the 63d St. "L" tracks where the dill pickles and hardboiled eggs were free, and if we went in together on a pitcher of beer, a plate of corned beef and cabbage was 45c. Our discussions of the discipline and politics of reading, whether an opinion by Justice Cardozo or a novel by Jane Austen, were often lengthy and intense. Everybody did a lot of listening, and the more I heard, the less intensely I came to feel about Cardozo's *ratio decidendi* and the more intrigued I became with Jane Austen's total artistry.

5.

Meanwhile, I was up to my ears in political activism as a member of Chicago's North Side Chapter of the American Veterans Committee. Anyone who didn't live through it would have a hard time imagining the excitement, hope, and anxiety of this brief political interlude, roughly 1945-1950, when a huge window of opportunity seemed open before America descended into its Cold War McCarthyism and buttoned-down 1950s. Already during the war, two highly influential Americans had articulated two opposite visions of the country's postwar future, Henry Luce's "American Century," first promulgated in Luce's *Life* magazine in 1941, and Henry Wallace's *The Century of the Common Man*, promulgated in Wallace's 1943 book of that title. Luce argued for what in fact has transpired, an aborted half-century of American economic, political, and military conquest that has imploded in the devastation of Iraq and the global disproportion between superfluous wealth for a few and grinding poverty for the many, including millions of Americans denied decent livelihood, healthcare, culture, and spirituality.

Henry Wallace, who in 1946 was ranked in public opinion polls as one of America's most admired men, argued for a cooperative postwar century in which the World War II Allies would invite other nations to join them in forming a single economic unit based on full employment in well paying jobs. Wallace believed that worldwide "prices, production, and purchasing power can be held in balance with each other, and the economic machine can be kept running steadily and smoothly" through the same kind of planning America had relied on in the New Deal and war effort. His vision was capitalist and not socialist, rooted in the anti- monopoly progressivism that his Republican family had shared with Theodore Roosevelt at the turn of the twentieth century. But even after the economic and political horrors of two world wars, this vision was dismissed as utopian, and meanwhile Luce's vision that prevailed has devolved into the utopian warfare of shock and awe, surge and drones.

But before all that came to pass, there was in post-World War II America first and foremost a feeling in the air of expanding material horizons following the years of Depression and war shortages that were all most of us knew. There was a pent-up demand for goods—apartments and clothes, home appliances and novels, automobiles and Broadway musicals—and some accumulated savings to buy them. My first postwar dress suit was a double-breasted pale gray whose color and zooty cut I didn't like. But peacetime production was just getting started, the suit was my size, and it was either that or nothing. My mother could afford a new car to replace our 1936 DeSoto, but this was out of the question until she bought a Pontiac in 1949. And when Bobby and I got married in mid-1948, it took a connection of her uncle's to land us a two-room apartment with a pull-down bed.

Inseparable from this consumer demand, there was also for many Americans an expanding political horizon. The Depression had politicized masses of people, and FDR's programs to provide jobs and food had reached deeply into the lives of millions. There was an embryonic sense of community in which we were all in this together, with only marginal material differences, and a corresponding impulse to keep it all going. A whole generation of men, and unprecedented numbers of women, had been soldiers in a citizen army joined in common purpose, and for millions of others the home-front production of armaments meant nationwide full employment. This new work force, which was highly unionized and included a huge influx of women and blacks, had accepted a no-strike pledge for the duration of the war, and 25 million people had taken payroll deductions to buy low-interest government bonds in support of the war effort.

They weren't ready to surrender without a fight either their new standard of living or their new political sense of purpose and belonging. They wanted to continue working at a decent wage in a peacetime economy even with the return of GIs to the workforce, and this meant (among other things) a shorter work week at full pay for at least the postwar transition. "Full Employment" became a nationwide slogan, and even into the 60s there was public discussion of a Guaranteed Annual Income. At one point President Nixon endorsed the idea, and the US House of Representatives actually passed a GAI proposal. Meanwhile, the years 1945-6 saw a nationwide wave of strikes in pursuit of such goals, whose momentum was abruptly halted in 1947 by the promulgation of the Truman Doctrine and the passage of the Taft-Hartley Act. This two-pronged counterattack by corporate capital began the process, still ongoing, of eating away people's hopes for economic security and political voice in an authentically democratic community.

The Truman Doctrine, which proclaimed America's right to pursue regime change in other countries by fair means or foul whenever that served our self-defined interests, was an early step in the Cold War. It was also a political stimulus to the economic growth of what President Eisenhower was soon to call "the military-industrial complex" as a fail-safe engine for ensuring corporate profit and dominance. This Guaranteed Annual Profit for military contractors required a denial not only of the demands workers were then making, but also of their ability to keep making such demands. That was accomplished by the Taft-Hartley Act, which limited the right to strike, made union organizing perilously difficult, and precipitated a 60-year decline in union membership and influence, with still no end in sight.

This summary is of course simplified, but I hope it can suggest something of the hope, good will, and anxiety that animated millions of Americans who took on the corporate/political establishment during those years. The American Veterans Committee, established as a thinking man's alternative to the American Legion, was in many respects a microcosm of the national struggle to realize people's postwar hopes. Founded by Charles Bolte, Jr. (soon to be a US congressman from Pennsylvania), AVC quickly attracted a sizeable liberal constituency, including such luminaries as FDR Jr., G. Mennen Williams (soon to be governor of Michigan), and Michael Straight (editor of *The New Republic*), along with a United Front assortment of populists, progressives, socialists, communists, and Trotskyists. But as the Cold War militarization of the economy proceeded, AVC's liberal centrists and radical leftists were soon at each other's throats in the national organization, at whose two annual conventions I was to get an eye-popping education.

Chicago's North Side Chapter included both constituencies but never became factionalized, and it survived the demise of the national organization by something like fifty years as the renamed North Side Veterans Club. I think there were two reasons for this. First, we were people from different walks of life who now became friends and brought baby-boom children to chapter picnics, and in this we resembled any local post of The American Legion. Second, the United Front practice of that era's political left actually functioned to keep us working together despite our avowed differences. In deciding whether to take a stand on some issue, we talked things through to see if we could find common ground. If we couldn't, then we didn't take a stand. But if we could, as when we agreed overwhelmingly that the Truman Doctrine was a betrayal of American principles and a threat to world democracy, we acted in unison. My first activist deed was to drive the old De Soto, decked out in banners, at the head of a 40-car motorcade the entire length of Chicago's Lake Shore Drive in protest of the Truman Doctrine. This opened my dossier in the files of the FBI and the Chicago Police Red Squad, but it unfortunately failed to derail the Truman Doctrine.

At one of our monthly chapter meetings (to which the men wore suits and ties and were accompanied by their wives), we were addressed by local candidates for public office. At another we were shown a film depicting the production of Mott's Apple Sauce from the nation's finest apples by the nation's most cheerful workers teetering on the nation's highest ladders so as to meet the highest quality standards. At another we debated whether to support the United Packinghouse Workers in their 1948 Chicago strike, and a majority voted no. So for a couple of sizzling summer days I went by myself to the stockyards for the first time ever in order to walk the picket line. This turned out to be scary, although there were no confrontations with scabs or the police. For one thing, the heat only sharpened the fabulous stockyard stench that was sickening to me but was everyday breathing to my fellow picketers. For another, these picketers were almost all black, and if in those days you'd lived your whole life on Chicago's North Side, you would never have experienced being the only white person in a mass of frightening blacks. There it was the other way around, just as it had been in the army, and here at the stockyards my racism unnerved me even when making common cause.

AVC's two national conventions in New York and Chicago were devoted to a bitter, knock-down fight between liberals and leftists over the direction the organization should take. According to the Cold War myth then being fabricated by conservatives, the communists and their fellow-travelers "infiltrated" honorable civic or political organizations and then, by a magical process nobody ever tried to explain, "duped" the unsuspecting adults in these organizations into following the Party Line. An influential group of liberals promptly embraced this myth and, with a rationale provided by Reinhold Niebuhr, the much-admired Protestant theologian, formed the Americans for Democratic Action as an anti-communist alternative to the United Front left. The AVC liberals were of this cohort, and, from what I saw at our national conventions, it was they and not the left who practiced dirty politics. The most influential leader of the AVC left was a New York lawyer named Morris Pottish, a tall, lean, sad-faced man who looked like a Jewish Abraham Lincoln. I didn't know whether he was a communist, but I don't think I was duped by his arguments, which, by the standards of the University of Chicago Law School, were more logical, informed, and compelling than those of his liberal opponents. But Charles Bolte, FDR Jr., and "Soapy" Williams soon made it clear that their overriding interest was in hijacking the national organization to serve their nascent political careers, in which they could not risk offending the corporate/political establishment. They tried every devious parliamentary tactic to derail agreement on anything except their pre-approved agenda, and when their tactics kept on not working, they sabotaged the national organization.

In witnessing these AVC debates, I acquired a lifelong respect for Roberts Rules of Order. Like many good rules, they can easily be perverted, and the AVC liberals were adept at perverting them so as to stifle discussion and frustrate consensus whenever they saw things weren't going their way. But Morris Pottish was not only an eloquent speaker; he was a master at using Roberts Rules for the purpose intended, to facilitate debate, to produce agreement when agreement was in fact possible, and to clarify the grounds for disagreement when disagreement was inevitable. When I became chairperson of the Ohio State English department thirty years later, I re-studied Roberts Rules and at department meetings tried to apply them as I had seen Morris Pottish do.

6.

My experiences in leading the motorcade, walking the picket line, watching the Mott's movie, and watching Morris Pottish exhibit a deeper probity than FDR Jr. or the future governor of Michigan, began to add up. Now for the first time I thought about becoming a communist, and early in 1949, I can't remember exactly, I was invited to do that by my closest friend in our AVC chapter. Perry Winokur was a big loving man with a booming voice and wall-shaking laugh who looked like a linebacker but was gentle as a lamb. His wife Evelyn was a delicate, small-boned woman, whose still tinier widowed mother they were also supporting. In those heady days, this son of factory workers had gone into business for himself, and I had helped him get started. He bought vending machines, and together on weekends we dollied and wrestled them into factory and warehouse lunchrooms and apartment house basements. Like some other communists I met in those years, Perry had a Midas touch in entrepeneurship but could never get comfortable with his capitalist success. When the vending machine business became a gold mine, he sold it and started something else from scratch, I don't remember what, and when that also succeeded, he moved on to become Midwest Distributor for Amana refrigerators and freezers.

Perry was anything but an intellectual, and he didn't try to dupe me with theoretical arguments. He simply said, in so many words, look, Julian, you see for yourself how America is threatening to go, so how in good conscience can you not become a communist? Nor did he try to twist my arm but, after bringing up the subject a second time, left me alone. He knew this was a big commitment that I'd better make with a whole heart and not be hurried into something I would later regret.

I joined the Party, and although later I became very frightened to remain a member during the McCarthy witch-hunt, I have never had ethical or political reason to regret the two-plus years I belonged to the CPUSA. Nowadays this needs some explaining, and while my party membership continued after I left Chicago, let me try to explain it all here. In its 1930s peak years, the CPUSA had an estimated 100,000 adult members, with an estimated additional 20,000 in the Young Communist League. Then the 1939 Hitler-Stalin Pact drove out large numbers of people, particularly intellectuals, many of whom went on to write reams of blowhard about "The God That Failed." But my gut feeling in the 40s, which has only become more informed and confident since, was that my responsibility is to America making its history, not the USSR making its. And what I'd seen of the Truman Doctrine and Taft-Hartley Act, the packinghouse wages and conditions of work, the Mott's Apple Sauce propaganda and the AVC's national politics, illustrated a whole lot of what Phil Epstein must have meant in our army conversations when he spoke of capitalism's metabolic expropriation of workers and antagonism to actual democracy.

As many former members have observed, the CPUSA was more nearly a movement than a party: our activism was invested less in the Party itself than in broader organizations like the trade unions, the Civil Rights Congress, or the Women's International League For Peace and Freedom, whose policies we were trying to influence. We were no more "infiltrating" these organizations than were their Democrat, Republican, Socialist, and libertarian constituencies who also sought to influence them. We were just one contending group, and in this regard I found our meetings in my neighborhood chapters ("cells") not terribly helpful.

We were from diverse walks of life and engaged in diverse political activities. We shared the lonely if uplifting long-term goal of ending class, gender, and racial oppression, but the short-term means for attempting this inevitably had to vary from one context to another, and we were all working in different contexts. So our allegedly sinister cell meetings to plot the overthrow of the US government were in fact hand-holding support sessions to remind us we had comrades in trying to do what millions of others were also trying to do—peaceably to influence our nation's politics and history.

What I found most rewarding were our periodic discussions of what the Party called "The Negro Question" and "The Woman Question." Long before the Civil Rights Movement or second-wave feminism, the CPUSA was virtually alone in recognizing race and gender as fundamental social problems, inseparable from class and each other, needing desperately to be addressed in America. The terms in which we addressed them were oversimplified—one theory we pursued was that American Negroes constituted a nation within a nation, since they were the majority population of the Black Belt with a language, religion, and music of their own, and therefore deserved a measure of political independence. But that theory's Stalinist reductions pale before the Ivy League idiocies of today's "nation building" theories that produce untold death and destruction but not yet a nation. Ours was a serious address to race in America, and it also made somebody like me newly aware of his personal racism when walking a picket line.

It was pretty much the same with The Woman Question, and while our discussions of that had little bearing on my political activity, they transformed my personal life. Bobby and I began our married life sharing the cooking and housework, which is not at all how our parents did it. We also began with her typing my papers until I soon got a manual called *Touch Typing Self-Taught*, worked at it half an hour a night until I was competent, and never looked back. This sharing continued in my two subsequent marriages, and I was an early supporter of Women's Studies at my university.

Our discussions of what I will call "The Class Question," on the other hand, were not very productive either politically or personally. Class struggle being the *raison d' etre* of any communist party, this may seem at first surprising. All I was able to understand at the time is that we were not industrial workers seeking influence in the trade unions but middle class students and professionals seeking influence among our own. The working class in its struggles may have been crucial to us, but we had no everyday contact with those struggles. It then took me decades to understand in addition that class is a very different phenomenon from race and gender, no matter how all three might "inflect" each other, and requires a different mode of understanding. There were books asking to be written about this, and 50 years later in retirement I finally understood enough to write one of them.

As for top-down orders from New York or Moscow, I never heard any. True, we were once asked by the Chicago leadership to devote one meeting to a discussion of the theoretical justification for revolutionary violence, and we promptly came to the Leninist conclusion that capitalists feeling threatened would always be the first to resort to violence. This conclusion has been validated time after time all over the world in the 60 years since that cell meeting, but during my time in the Party I never met a communist, except for Perry Winokur that intrepid entrepreneur, who knew one end of a gun from the other.

My most memorable experience during my entire membership in the CPUSA was the Chicago party's 1949 Fourth of July picnic. This was held on several acres far out on the southwest side, where the police could not find excuses to hassle us and where every ethnicity in the city had a booth serving authentic food. Only in Cuba 50 years later have I seen a wider spectrum of skin colors, physiognomies, and clothing styles, or heard more varieties of speech, than we did among the thousands at that picnic. Bobby and I ate, then listened to live music, then ate, then listened to boring speeches, then ate, then learned a little folk dancing, and then ate. I'd lost twenty pounds since leaving the army, but that road ended here.

7.

The currents of my life had converged in my marriage to Bobby Stone in June, 1948. Her stepfather had been a client of my father's whose servant lit the cigars, and who also declined to support Bobby and her sister when he married their widowed mother. A year-and-a-half younger than I, she was now on her own and groping at life much as I was. In retrospect I think we were both lonely at heart while trying to get free of our mothers, and we found some bonding in that. We were also unused to physical intimacy, and our first times at sex were awkwardly inept. We got better at that, and out of bed we supported and extended each other in any number of ways. Bobby's literary friends and aspirations made my new interest in literature feel less academic, and my political intensity and public aplomb may have made her feel more safe. She was (and is) a great comic mime where I am soberly forensic, and her zany intuitiveness was a balance to my sedate logic. We both had a lot of good will overlying our neuroses, yet despite constantly renewed efforts at mutual support, we finally grew apart. Our marriage lasted 13 years, and our two children had to find their way into life through the hurt we entailed on them.

But all that was to come later, and our immediate horizon was full of excitement. Bobby was friends with Stuart Brent, whose Seven Stairs Bookshop on the Magnificent Mile was a postwar Chicago literary institution. Stuart hosted readings, lectures, and signings, at which we met Algren, Conroy, Motley, and others. We talked most often with Jack Conroy, who was now the *Sun-Times'* chief book-reviewer, and this led once to his inviting us to his home. Jack's first book, *The Disinherited*, was a celebrated proletarian novel of the 30s, and during that decade he had also been editor of the Midwest left's leading literary magazines, *The Anvil* and *The New Anvil*. His ramshackle clapboard house in Chicago's Irish section was not easy to single out, and our first view upon entering was of Mrs. Conroy sitting at the kitchen table in a cotton print dress staring at her beer bottle— right out of a Walker Evans photograph. But what Jack had invited us out to see was not his wife but the new floor-to-ceiling bookcases made by his reformed alcoholic son. To hear Jack talk, those bookcases meant everything to him, and what we saw coincidentally on their shelves were rows of books by Nelson Algren, Millen Brand, Erskine Caldwell, William Faulkner, Langston Hughes, Meridel Le Sueur, and Richard Wright (among others), one after another inscribed to Jack with thanks for publishing the writer's earliest work in *The Anvil* or *New Anvil*. The most frequent and grateful inscriber appeared to be William Faulkner.

Bobby's still closer friends were Jayne and Alwyn Berland, who welcomed me immediately into their lives. Jayne was a poet, Al was a graduate student in English at the university, both were communists at the time, and both were knowledgeable lovers of classical music. They were a few years older than we, and they had an infant son Kerry, whom we sometimes babysat. We talked poetry, politics, and Beethoven at their apartment, and I began picking up Al in the De Soto on my daily route to the university. It was something like a half hour's drive from his place, during which Al would often talk about his courses and teachers in the English department This was the heyday of the "Chicago neo-Aristotelians," and Al's description of their theory and pedagogy picked up where last year's lunches left off in arousing my interest in literary study. These Aristotelians were committed not only to the close reading of texts but also and inseparably to poetics itself, to developing a comprehensive theory of literary genres, purposes, and emotional effects. And for some of them, this commitment entailed the Socratic dialogue in the classroom which had made Levi's law course so absorbing.

Al Berland also introduced me to the music criticism of B.H. Haggin, which turned out to be a lasting influence on my intellectual life. It's not too much to say that in endlessly re-reading Haggin I learned not only how to listen to music but also how to write literary criticism. From *A Book of the Symphony* in 1938 to *Music For the Man Who Enjoys 'Hamlet'* in 1944 to *The*

New Listener's Musical Companion in 1991, Haggin's practice in a half-dozen books was to analyze musical works and performances for their structures, progressions, and emotional effects, in a manner parallel to that of the literary Aristotelians, and to communicate his insights in non-technical language that a layperson reading on the "L" could comprehend. Like his great predecessors Hector Berlioz and George Bernard Shaw, Haggin was a working journalist who needed to be both clear and succinct, and when I first attempted literary criticism I had a Haggin-inspired sign taped to the wall above my typewriter: NO BULLSHIT. But it is taking me forever to learn that lesson.

During these years my sister Mimi was finishing high school at Frances Shimer in Missouri, and my brother Chuck, following a stint in the postwar army, was at Harvard Law School, where he set records for winning at Monopoly as extracurricular relaxation. My mother and I saw the Chicago premiers of *The Glass Menagerie* and Paul Robeson's *Othello*, and I joined a group transfixed on the sidewalk before a store window displaying the first LP records spinning at an excruciatingly slow 33rpm. I was also a poll watcher for Henry Wallace's Progressive Party in the 1948 presidential election, where, at a near west side precinct, I observed Mayor Daley's minions distributing $2 bills and marked ballots to the dozens of winos they'd rounded up from Skid Row.

Bobby and I saw Mike Nichols and Elaine May at the Second City comedy club, and with my mother and Mimi we saw Paul Leder perform in the road company chorus line of *Top Banana*, a wildly misogynist Phil Silvers musical. Paul was now married to a concentration camp survivor with a tattooed number on her wrist, and Ethel had come with him and their new son to Chicago. She and Reuben were staying in a seedy hotel around the corner from the theater, and we spent evenings waiting up with her until Paul got home. That turned out to be the last time we saw each other. After a couple more years of struggle on Broadway, Paul moved his family to Los Angeles, where he became an admired independent filmmaker and all three of his children made careers in the film industry. We exchanged a few letters and then - lost touch.

Another buddy from the 84th came to Chicago as an offensive lineman with the Baltimore Colts for a game with our

Bears. Mike Phillips was a western Pennsylvania football player with only one eye, and so the army had made him a truck driver. He'd driven us through Aachen to Buchenwald over some horrendous roads, and whenever he wasn't driving was ready to help out in the 84th any way he could. Now he bought me a steak dinner at the Palmer House, where the Colts were staying, but I remember our reunion as more wistful than happy. Tough as he was both mentally and physically, Mike knew he was undersized for an offensive lineman, not to mention lacking in peripheral vision. He knew he'd be playing for only an interim while the NFL replenished its personnel, and beyond that he had no ambitions, qualifications, or prospects. Flush for the moment with money and status, he was also a bit forlorn.

So it was that the 84th faded into memory just when the new alchemy of my relations with Bobby, the Berlands, and B.H. Haggin led me to quit law school and break with my father's memory after the first quarter of my sophomore year. In fact, I'd had an early warning signal that something like this might be coming. At the end of the freshman year I'd had a huge panic on the night before taking my final exams. All the freshman courses had been year-long, with no periodic quizzes to let you know how you were doing, and then we had a gruesome week of exams covering the entire year's work in each course. This arrangement was of course not conducive to calm for anybody, but my upset o'erflowed the measure. On the night before the round of exams began, I was up all night writhing in anxiety while drinking as much bourbon as my body could tolerate. It wasn't as if I hadn't studied well, and in fact I passed the exams with respectable, if undistinguished, grades. I faltered only in Negotiable Instruments, where the entire four-hour exam consisted of a single dense question about a bounced check, or something like that. Only the commercial masterminds in our class answered this question well, and I believe the rest of us got credit just for intelligently trying.

I'd had a vague sense at the time that my panic attack might be telling me something. It went so far beyond any exam jitters I'd experienced before as to make me wonder if it were a signal that the law was finally not for me. But I returned unhesitatingly for my sophomore year, and that's when I began driving Al Berland to school. In retrospect I believe my night of panic involved a rejection of my father as role-model no matter how much I admired him, and in this rejection I also knew I was giving up the possibility of a career connected immediately with politics. But there was now someplace else I really wanted to go after all my writhings. I applied and was accepted for graduate study in English at Chicago and, with a lot of excitement and anxiety, embarked on what turned out to be my vocation.

CHAPTER 3. A SCATTERSHOT APPRENTICESHIP:

CHICAGO/MINNEAPOLIS, 1949-1956

Back in Madison the summer before entering the army, I'd taken the British lit. survey course from a marvelous teacher, scholar, and *hora* dancer, Professor Ruth Wallerstein, who once took me to lunch and urged me to major in English. Now that I was following her advice six years later in Chicago, I felt completely lost in writing my first full-length term paper for a course on Spenser and Milton. All I could do was ask myself how Professor Sirluck had to think in order to say what he said in class, and then try to mimic him. Bobby typed the paper I managed to write, it got an A-, and that gave me the courage to go on.

Then among my subsequent courses were two with the touted neo-Aristotelians, The Analysis of Arguments with Elder Olson and Shakespeare with William Rea Keast. Olson, who was one of the group's leading theorists, had us spend the entire quarter dissecting Hume's *Enquiry Concerning Human Understanding*, and he was an awful classroom teacher who proceeded strictly by question-and-answer but never asked a question besides "Guess what I'm thinking?" Keast on the other hand was a terrific Socratic teacher, for no matter what answer you might give a question, he could follow it with another that led you to think further into the structure, progression, and emotional effect of each individual play. There was even so a catch to this, for Keast's questions invariably led us back into his Aristotelian train of thought, and as we saw this keep happening, a couple of us tried to bedevil him with answers deliberately calculated to derail the train. But we couldn't do it: the more perversely ingenious we became, the more adroitly he outflanked us, so that for Keast in the long run, just as for Olson, our answers to his questions had to reach a foregone conclusion. But where Olson dragged you through a disjointed guessing game, which I knew I'd want to avoid if I got to be in his

57

position, Keast caught you up in a dynamic process of thought, which I saw was something to build on.

The excitement of Keast's pedagogy in teaching Shakespeare, following Levi's in teaching the philosophy of law, is the deepest legacy of my experience at Chicago (besides the Beethoven late quartet cycle performed over three nights by the Budapest String Quartet at the height of its glory). It impelled me toward years of reflection on teaching, in which I'd begun by adopting a stupid distinction between lecture and discussion classes: lectures give you what you can read in a book anyway, whereas discussion really gets you thinking. Yet amidst much dreary lecturing at Chicago, I'd also heard some finely wrought, tip-of-the-iceberg syntheses that drew on years of study and reflection, including one by the nuclear physicist Enrico Fermi, who traced a giant atom on the chalkboard, put a question-mark in the middle, and then for a riveting hour explained everything you need to know about atomic fission. I'd also suffered through a lot of tedious discussion that was either a guessing game like Olson's at what the teacher was thinking, or else a free-for-all that led nowhere. The professor in one psychology course was a disciple of Carl Rogers, Chicago's famed exponent of "non-directive therapy," and at our first class meeting he applied his mentor's theory by remaining steadfastly silent, which set the tone for an entire term in which we wandered in every direction without ever a clue.

What got under my skin about Keast's teaching was the way his questions drew you into a step-by-step, problem-solving progression in which you weighed alternatives and anticipated objections at each step, and then felt compelled by the steps you had taken to come out where he wanted you to. Back then I could at least sense the possibility of pushing the discussion further by formulating questions that would produce a similarly coherent progression yet also leave the teacher open to learning from her students and arriving with delight at some unexpected place. But it took another decade before I became capable of such questions.

It made a huge difference, of course, that Keast was doing all this with Shakespeare's plays, which invite a more complex analysis than Aristotle's analysis of Aeschylus and Sophocles. But then Shakespeare is like that—he can deepen both your aesthetic pleasure and your knowledge of life the more you attend to him, and here is my other big legacy from Chicago. Shakespeare responds not only to Aristotelian but to every kind of analysis because this white male Eurocentric is in fact a greater writer than almost everybody else. His plays, like Beethoven's quartets, take us out of ourselves and return us enlarged for life beyond personal identity as few human creations have done, and I felt in them a power of thought and feeling that transcends everybody's politics.

In the vocabulary of today's cultural politics, the word "aesthetic" has been transmogrified from an elitist to an egalitarian adjective that describes just one of the art work's many features— "thematic," "rhetorical," "ethical"—all of which "inflect" one other but none of which is "privileged" above the others. This vocabulary makes difficult any reasoned argument for what I felt then, and have felt ever since, as the individual greatness of particular works of art. I was a card-carrying communist when I studied Shakespeare with Keast, and I certainly found in the plays food for marxist thought. But while I was to argue years later for the aesthetic power of *King Lear* as specifically a marxian tragedy, I also saw back then that Shakespeare's plays for the most part are not overtly political and yet dwarf in knowledge, feeling, and power almost all works that are. I came to identify *King Lear*'s marxism in the ideological conflict that structures the play, between Edmund with his allies and Cordelia with hers. But this conflict would leave us cold if Shakespeare did not embed it in his characters' everyday desire for recognition and justice, along with their different forms of love for one another, through the process of his art. His ability to humanize ideas through structure and style is equally evident in other plays, and it led my aestheticism to become a condition for my marxism. That also kept me from falling into political ecstasy every time I saw a passage of social protest congenial to marxism in the world literature I later read.

2.

Once Bobby and I had an apartment of our own, with rent to pay and furnishings to buy, we needed more money than her secretary's salary and my GI Bill stipend. So I got a part-time job at a Kosher delicatessen in the heart of Hyde Park, halfway between the university and our apartment on the corner of 47th &

Ellis. This was an old story for me: in high school I had a noon-hour cooking job in one of those hole-in-the-wall lunch places, and in Madison during my freshman year I worked the afternoon shift on the grill of a campus diner. But this deli was the best yet. Every day we made fresh chopped liver, potato salad, and cole slaw; we fished giant dill pickles from a wooden barrel; we had a fine-tuned machine for slicing the great briskets of corned beef and pastrami; and our centerpiece behind the counter was a wood-block table on which lay in splendor an 18-pound smoked salmon filet, give or take an ounce. From this we sliced lox with a lethal knife about two feet long, and once I stopped musing about Shakespeare while slitting my finger with this knife, I was able to produce paper-thin slices to layer on freshly cut bagels spread with just the amount of cream cheese the peering customer would like. Our best-selling soft drink was cream soda.

Living now on Chicago's South Side, we encountered black people daily for the first time in our lives, but this didn't get me past the fear I'd felt among them on the packinghouse picket line. In fact, I was all but traumatized by one indelible episode. Through our CP cell we became friends with the artist Bernard Goss, a sharply intelligent, handsome black man full of energy who everyone called "Goss," and his white partner, Rose Schwartz, a plain and pained woman with an air of martyring herself to an interracial ideal. Chicago was probably even then what Martin Luther King later called the most segregated city in the North, and we lived just a few blocks from the boundary of its huge South Side ghetto. I could hide my tension when Goss and Rose came to dinner at our apartment, but not when we went to theirs. They lived on South Park Avenue, a grand boulevard with islands down the middle and block after block of palatial homes long abandoned by Chicago's white aristocracy and now subdivided *ad nauseam* into warrens for black people. After getting off the streetcar, Bobbie and I had to walk three or four blocks to Goss's address on a lovely spring evening when crowds were strolling the sidewalks strewn with litter. Not a person among them was white in the endless vista ahead, and I was sure we'd be assaulted any minute. When we arrived, Goss must have seen my pallor, and he tried to calm me by inviting me to accompany him on a quick errand while Bobbie helped Rose make the salad. We walked a couple of blocks to a smoke-filled pool hall for which he was to do sign-painting, and when everybody stopped playing to stare at me with their cues leveled like bayonets, I just about froze. Bobbie said later that Rose's dinner was terrific, but I can't remember tasting a thing.

The taste I remember is of the Chinese food at a restaurant on The Midway called "The Tropical Hut," where Al Berland and I had lunch on the rare occasions when we felt flush. Now I had my own stories to tell about Keast's and Olson's classes, and the more we talked, the more certain I became that I wanted to follow Al in specializing in American literature for my Ph.D.. Here my politics trumped my aesthetics in the first of many oscillations over the coming years. I knew of course that American writers had written some aesthetically exciting works, but I was mostly eager to study the interrelations of economics, politics, and literature in the history of my own nation. This being the case, Al urged me not to do the Ph.D. with the professors he'd had at Chicago, but to go to Minnesota, which had assembled an exceptional faculty in American literature and established the country's first Ph.D. program in American Studies. When I ventured to discuss this with Professor Keast, he urged me to stay, but then I took my first American literature course with Professor Blair, who turned out to be a bore. Al and Jayne would be moving to Iowa, where he'd got an ABD job, and I applied and was accepted to the Ph.D. program at Minnesota.

3.

The University of Minnesota was at that time an academic and cultural mecca. Twin City natives used to say, "We have two seasons here, winter and the Fourth of July," and this may explain their exceptional town-and-gown culture. Those people didn't hibernate; at -15 they'd say, "It's a dry cold," and go off to a Minneapolis Symphony concert at its home auditorium on the university campus. The conductor was Antal Dorati, whose Mercury recordings remain staples even now, and who organized summer festivals where you could hear for a pittance over three evenings all six of Bach's Brandenburg Concertos, or Mozart's six violin concertos performed by the internationally renowned Szymon Goldberg.

The university could barely meet its demand for evening classes, and I was later to teach my first Shakespeare course to adults coming directly from work. The *Star and Tribune*'s nationally syndicated columnist, Carl Rowan, was guest professor of journalism, Hubert Humphrey and Eugene McCarthy were guest lecturers in political science, and there were researchers in the medical school whose unheard of specialty was preventive medicine and public health. Just across town the Walker Art Center was thought by many to be second for modern art only to MoMa.

The center of literary ferment in all this was the university's General College, a two-year, bonehead college for students whose high school records made them inadmissible to the university. They were not thought to require Ph.D.-credentialed faculty, and the General College faculty had become a magnet for mavericks like my friend Norman Sherman, who was soon to become Humphrey's long-time press secretary, along with newly blossoming writers like Saul Bellow, John Berryman, and Isaac Rosenfeld at the time I arrived. Some of these taught occasionally in the English department in relief of Robert Penn Warren, but after my first year both Bellow and Warren left and I never got to take them.

That hardly mattered in the embarrassment of riches now before me. Minnesota's American Literature faculty was triple the size of Chicago's and included two exceptional teachers—Leo Marx and Henry Nash Smith, very different in style but both inspiring. They were then writing their groundbreaking books in American Studies, Smith's *Virgin Land: The American West as Symbol and Myth* and Marx's *The Machine in the Garden: Technology and the Pastoral Ideal in America*, and Smith was also elaborating in his Mark Twain seminar the "vernacular/genteel" distinction he'd inferred from Chaucer's *Canterbury Tales*.

The breadth and depth of the American literature faculty went far beyond my expectations, and if it had been for them alone, I might have taken my Ph.D in American Studies. But other English faculty were also exceptional, and I wasn't ready to foreclose the intellectual possibilities opened by three of these, Samuel Monk, David Erdman, and Allen Tate, with each of whom I took a year-long course. Monk's lectures on eighteenth-century

British literature, day in and day out, were lapidary gems that ended just when the bell rang and were the greatest I've ever heard. I knew in advance that his stiff-necked century would be temperamentally alien to me, but following Monk in detail as he wove his great tapestry of Pope and Newton, Swift and Defoe, Dr. Johnson and Hume, Hogarth and Mozart, was itself an adventure in the life of the mind. In the nineteenth-century course I was Erdman's teaching assistant, and he was Monk's opposite in the classroom—a herky-jerky lecturer who thought on his feet and always seemed just a step behind his material. But he was also a path-breaking marxist some of whose material was the book he was then writing, *Blake, Prophet Against Empire*, which failed to earn him tenure at Minnesota but became an instant classic of historical scholarship.

Allen Tate was one of a kind: a small-boned, opinionated Southerner with a head too big for his body, also a poet, literary critic, sparkling conversationalist, and amateur violinist whose wife, the novelist Caroline Gordon, took enormous pride in the welsh rarebits she cooked for our seminar in literary theory. Tate's politics couldn't be more opposite to Erdman's: his most famous poem is "Ode to the Confederate Dead," and the bristling title of his current book was *Reactionary Essays on Poetry and Ideas*. But he was a public intellectual who could listen as well as talk, and whose talk was never more scintillating than when he was in his cups. Once at a Walker Art Center reception, Tate slowly collapsed to the floor, martini in hand, in the midst of a circle gathered round him and the middle of a sentence endorsing T.S. Eliot's argument for a Christian society. As two of us lifted him gently back to his feet, he went right on without skipping a word.

Tate was among the founders of the New Criticism, which was then entering its dominance of American literary studies with its pedagogical program of "close reading"—the analysis of literary texts neither as historical reflections of their authors' lives and times, nor as thematic vehicles for their authors' political or religious ideas, but as purposefully structured, internally coherent works that are aesthetically satisfying and valuable in and for themselves. T.S. Eliot, the movement's chief spokesman, famously said that a poem is a poem and not some other thing, and that

Henry James had a mind so fine that no idea could violate it. In the 1950s the New Critics were criticized by Chicago's Aristotelians for misconceiving literature as a specialized form of language, and while they survived this theoretical critique, they succumbed in the mid-60s to political attack for espousing an elitist aestheticism that ignored the literary travails of race, gender, and class. But I experienced The New Criticism as enormously liberating, both pedagogically and politically, and nowadays perhaps this also needs explaining.

Most of the unexceptional professors I had at Chicago and Minnesota taught from the assumption that a literary text could be understood only by reference to its historical "background" of facts about the author's life and cultural *milieu*. These historical facts, unlike the texts we were reading, were inaccessible in the classroom. They had to be imported from the library in the form of the professor's lectures, which, even when these were as dazzling as Samuel Monk's, made the classroom a site of passive note-taking rather than active thinking. Here the difference between lecture and discussion was not a personal accident of professorial style but an organic requirement of the subject matter, and our occasional "discussion" hours were only for the sake of asking clarification about what we'd heard in lecture.

What the New Criticism made widely possible was a communal, problem-solving process of teacher and students thinking a text through together in the here and now of the classroom. It was not as if the New Critics ignored biographical or historical information that could in fact be instrumental to understanding the text; they just wanted to keep it at that while keeping focused on the text. In so doing, they were open to hearing from their students, who could often see things they had missed (and some things no sane person would think of). Allen Tate was not only the most opinionated teacher I ever had, but also one of the two or three best listeners. He could learn from us every day in the classroom as neither Keast nor Monk could do, nor even perhaps those later theorists of identity, structure, and power whose -isms and post-isms displaced the New Criticism.

The great teacher at Minnesota who brought all this together for me was Henry Nash Smith, who could say in an aside, "I am incurably historically minded," while also analyzing the text before him just as subtly as Allen Tate. I was far from alone in worshipping Smith: he was a scholar-teacher hero to a generation of Minnesota students in American literature and American Studies. What made him so for me was his focus on the text's interaction with its historical background as actively contributing to its aesthetic form and emotional effect. For Smith the literary work and its background mutually shape each other, and their reciprocity was nowhere more evident than in the works of Mark Twain, Smith's defining subject of study just as Shakespeare was Keast's. Smith's close reading showed us how the narrative conflicts of Twain's fiction—in   dialect, ethics, morality, religion—between the "two ways of looking at the world" that Smith called "vernacular" and "genteel," define both his successes and his failures as a literary artist. Smith then also showed, through his deep knowledge of American history and culture, how Twain's successes and failures directly influenced the nation's identity-shaping conflict between seaboard and frontier as entire ways of life.

This was not marxism, but its manner of coupling aesthetic form with ideological content was compelling to someone like me who didn't want to sacrifice one to the other. It was far more persuasive than the one-dimensional marxist criticism I then knew, which was a crude variation on the "historical background" approach to literary study. So it was that unbeknownst to Smith, I went on talking with him inside my head for thirty years while I stumbled toward a marxist literary theory we might both find persuasive. He once told a group of us graduate students that an occupational feature of teaching is that the good you do only shows up after the course is over and seldom gets back to you. I've had it get back to me thirty years later, but Henry Smith died in an auto accident before I could let myself tell him.

I wish I could have told him two things especially. The first is that his two grand analyses, of cultural symbols that influenced the settlement of the American West, and of Mark Twain's struggle to resolve his vernacular/genteel conflict, weaned me from the marxian theory of base and superstructure as a means to explain the relation of culture to society. Smith demonstrated in *Virgin Land* how the Jeffersonian symbol of America as "The

Garden of the World" was no less influential than Appalachian poverty in motivating people to settle the Dust Bowl after reading real estate brochures proclaiming that "rain follows the plow." In this as in many examples throughout *Virgin Land*, it would be impossible for a marxist to say whether the base or the superstructure is the chicken or the egg.

Smith's work on Mark Twain also demonstrated how Twain's effort to resolve his vernacular/genteel conflict by making Hank Morgan, the hero of *A Connecticut Yankee in King Arthur's Court*, both a vernacular descendant of Huckleberry Finn and a successful capitalist entrepreneur was a huge artistic failure that foretold the bitter nihilism of Twain's final years. In this as in many examples from Smith's writing on Twain, the work of art is a battleground of class conflict within human consciousness, and watching this conflict unfold in the formal processes of art makes it difficult to regard the work of consciousness as simply the superstructural reflection of an economic base.

Besides thanking Smith for freeing me from that marxian metaphor, I wish I could have persuaded him that his then courageous use of the word "capitalism" nevertheless failed to embrace the marxian concept of expropriation. It took me some more years to see that when marxism is stripped to its essentials, it rests on a single, two-fold conception—first, that capitalism, like slavery and feudalism, is a social process wherein workers are required to produce more than they need for subsistence and their surplus is appropriated by others without their consent; and second, that unlike slavery or feudalism, capitalism has a built-in need to keep maximizing this surplus—"as if," in Hamlet's words, "increase of appetite grows by what it feeds on." Once I saw this, not only would I have liked to persuade Smith of it, but also to persuade him that writers like Shakespeare and Dickens, Henry James and Barbara Kingsolver, reached this understanding of capitalism through the formal process of their art, whereas Twain's formal breakdown in *A Connecticut Yankee* reflects among other things his failure to reach it

4.

During our seven years in Minneapolis, Bobby and I lived in four rental units, in one of which I had to order each winter's coal, start the fire every morning, replenish it twice a day, and bank it at night before going to bed. When we had to find a bigger place after our second child was born, I helped a skinflint Norwegian landlord rehab an old house in return for nominal rent, and when we'd finished re-wiring, re-plumbing, painting the walls, and tiling the floors while living in the house, he quadrupled the rent and we had to move again.

We also developed during these years a network of friends among graduate students and a few CP comrades, with some occasional overlapping. The University of Minnesota attracted at that time a surprising number of bright New York Jews who dared to cross the Hudson in order to enlarge their minds. Among them was the physicist Bill Cohen, with whom four of us had an agreement that on any morning when the temperature was -20 or colder, he would drive his model-T to each of our apartments and start our cars with his battery cables. We became particular friends with Anne Halley and Jules Chametzky, who were married in our apartment and proceeded to have children in tandem with ours. Anne's parents and two siblings were all M.D.'s, and, as a budding poet and student of literature, she was the family sore thumb. Jules's father was a Brooklyn kosher butcher, his street friends growing up were Stanley Kubrick and Norman Podhoretz, and he was to become a noted scholar of American Jewish literature as well as founder and long-time editor of *The Massachusetts Review*.

Jules and Anne introduced us to Jerome Liebling and his wife Phyllis, who were producing babies even faster than we were, and we six mingled our kids, groceries, and ideas week in and week out for five years. Jerry was the Department of Art's lone photographer and lowliest member, and by the time Jules and I got our Ph.D.'s, he also moved on to establish the legendary program in photography at Hampshire College, where he mentored Ken Burns (among others) while also becoming recognized internationally for the artist he is.

Our favorite joint stroller expedition was to a butcher shop at Seven Corners offering every USDA grade of meat from "prime" and "choice" through "restaurant" and "utility." Like kids in a candy store, we gaped at "choice" but mostly bought "utility." On Friday afternoons we hung out with other graduate students in Dinkytown, the university's commercial block, whose hub was

McCosh's used book store, owned by a graduate school dropout, premature hippie, and learned bibliophile whose shelves were stocked with books especially appealing to students of history and literature. McCosh's woodstove was hot, his prices were modest, and he was incapable of conversation about anything besides editions, printings, and bindings. So we ignored him and talked among ourselves about our teachers and their ideas.

Bobby's and my other great friend was the communist writer Meridel Le Sueur. Like Allen Tate, Meridel was an original; unlike him, she was larger than life and beggars description. Much of her fiction is informed by the Demeter myth, and I've always thought of her as an earth mother looking to sow her seeds everywhere. In her younger days as an aspiring actress, she was turned down by Hollywood for refusing to have her Semitic nose surgically repaired, and then again for the radio part of Betty Crocker because her voice was too sexy for the kitchen. Now in middle age, with two grown children and two grandchildren whom she babysat with our two, Meridel was a stunning woman whose dignity and spirit Jerry Liebling found a way to capture in his photographs. She lived part of each year on an Indian reservation (her great-grandmother was an Iroquois), and, just when her publication outlets were drying up in this heyday of anti-communism, she and her daughters were relentlessly hounded by the FBI, which deemed it periodically necessary to our national security to deflate their automobile tires.

But none of that distracted Meridel from talking intently with Bobby and me about Bobby's writing, or the books one or another of us was reading, and when I sent her years later my first published article, on the form of Dreiser's storytelling, she wrote me a detailed letter suggesting further implications of my argument. Yet all the time I knew her, I silently condescended to Meridel's fiction, which just wasn't up the aesthetic standard set by Shakespeare, Jane Austen, and Henry James. For all that I was learning from Henry Smith, I was still compartmentalizing my literary and political interests, and it was only after Meridel's death that I began to understand her struggle as a proletarian feminist writer in the way he understood Mark Twain's struggle as a vernacular writer. I then tried to honor her with a chapter in *The Marxian Imagination*.

5.

These were the years of the Korean War and political hysteria of McCarthyism, those toxic first fruits of the Truman Doctrine, and during these years my commitment to the Communist Party pretty much evaporated. For one thing, the Twin Cities party was much smaller, less active, and less theoretically capable than the Chicago party; our discussions at meetings were mostly unedifying, and our attempts to mobilize protest were mostly token. I joined with a Trotskyist fellow graduate student, David Hereshoff, in organizing a protest committee on behalf of a black philosophy instructor who had been denied tenure by his department. We were quick to suspect that racism was involved, and we made some serious noise. But the decision stood, and now in retrospect I doubt it was racism. The philosophy department's stars at that time were the renowned logical positivists Herbert Feigl and Wilfred Sellars, and my guess is that Forrest Wiggins' philosophical commitments just weren't in tune with theirs.

I was also instrumental in landing a big left-wing cultural event for the Minneapolis Symphony's campus auditorium. Through a violinist friend in the symphony, I got in touch with a blacklisted Chicago disc jockey, Studs Terkel, and arranged for him to come north with his trio of folk singers, Big Bill Broonzy, Win Stracke, and Blind Sonny Terry. Studs sat on the front edge of the stage with legs dangling over and mike in hand, and his inimitable commentary enriched a sparkling performance before a sellout crowd.

Yet despite this sporadic activism, I felt an increasing split between the world of the party and the world of the university. Meridel worried that I might desert marxism for the ivory tower, but despite our common interests, the vocation I aspired to was different from hers. In 1938 she had written in her journal, "It isn't any wonder people feel religious about the party. It is love, wife, and children to us." She was then at odds with the party's literary gurus, all male, who criticized her stories as too feminist and her style as too lyrical. But they and others kept publishing her work, which was also funded for a time by the Federal Writers Project, so that she could support herself if barely, and at least for stretches, by practicing her vocation while contending with her critics. She remained a party member for the rest of her 96 years and repeatedly told interviewers that the party had been "nourishing" to her.

It had also been nourishing to me until now, but my experience in the classrooms of Levi and Keast, Monk and Tate, Marx and Smith, had deepened my desire to become a professor, and my first experiences as a teaching assistant had confirmed me in this desire. At Chicago I'd taken a couple of education courses, so as to qualify to teach high school if I didn't prove good enough to get a Ph.D., and now that I was getting the Ph.D., university teaching was my ambition. But even beyond that, I felt that the opportunity to cultivate marxist thinking was also best taken in the university, and here we come to a marxian shibboleth about the divorce between mental and manual labor.

It is certainly true that the basic division of labor under capitalism, in which capitalists and their managers do the mental work and workers and their families do the physical, alienates everyone concerned from their products, their environment, and each other. It dumbs everybody down in regard to life's possibilities except great wealth with little meaning for a few and bare livelihood with little meaning for too many. It is also true that socialism can make physical labor less wearing by such devices as job rotation, considerate scheduling, sick and maternity leave, and extended vacations. But I don't think it follows from all this that human fulfillment for each of us individually, the supreme goal of socialism, requires some kind of balance between mental and manual labor. Marx imagined an ideal world in which, as he put it, we can each work in the morning, write poetry in the afternoon, and go fishing after dinner (or vice versa). But as Mozart once wrote in a letter, "I write music the way a cow shits," and I have to think this was also true for Teresa Edwards playing basketball, Enrico Fermi doing physics, Maria-Joao Pires at her piano, and Picasso at his easel. I can't imagine Edwards stunting her kinesthetic intelligence by taking time off to study sociology, or Picasso his imagination by bending over to cut sugar cane. Some people live though their bodies, some through their minds, and some (like me) through both. My desire to become a professor was also a desire to keep on studying, and although my old friend Putch has reminded me that already back in the army I was (fatuously) calling myself an intellectual, only now was I beginning to see that I wanted to live my whole life for the sake of ideas.

Even so, I stuck with the Party for over a year after I stopped participating, just to bear witness against McCarthyism as a matter of principle. Although I was regularly frightened into sleepless nights by the latest episode in the witch hunt, I couldn't accept the appearance of quitting out of fear. The Minnesota state legislature, like others, had established its own un-American activities committee to investigate subversives, and a woman who'd been a member of our CP cell volunteered to appear before this committee and name names. But instead of fingering me, Bobby, or any other CP member except her estranged husband, she named two non-members with conspicuously Jewish names, my friends Gene Bluestein and Jules Chametzky. Like me, they were both teaching assistants paid with state funds, and they were now subjected for months to telephone crank calls that included death threats. But the university stood firm, the hubbub died down, Gene and Jules proceeded, and I felt guilty.

Yet the McCarthy terror didn't keep me from studying marxism sporadically when the opportunity offered. Well before the advent of McCarthyism, many people had left the party for reasons similar to mine and, in so doing, had also given up on marxism itself. But I remained hooked. I knew a lot more now than I did when Perry Winokur asked me back in Chicago how in good conscience I could not be a communist, and my marxian conscience had only deepened with what I'd learned about workers' surplus labor being appropriated for millennia without their consent by slave owners, lords, kings, and CEOs. This marxian knowledge had become for me, all but insensibly, impervious to both the failures of the Communist party and the savagery of the McCarthy Inquisition.

My minor field for the Ph.D. was American history, where by far the two best courses I took were devoted to America's religious and socialist utopian communities of the 1840s and 1850s, and America's "Gilded Age" of economic rapacity and political corruption in securing the expropriation of workers' surplus labor following the Civil War. It was as if the pre-war socialists foresaw what was coming when they tried to create self-sustaining communities imbued with a culture of mutual aid instead of the dog-eat-dog culture that triumphed with American capitalism. But I couldn't see as yet how to connect any of this with imaginative literature except in superficial ways. Our literature is full of fiction that depicts in monochromatic detail the injustices of slavery, patriarchy, and capitalism as experienced in the daily lives of their victims—*Uncle Tom's Cabin, The Yellow Wallpaper, The Jungle.* But few actual lives are lived simply and solely as victimization, nor did any of the fiction I knew connect victimization specifically to surplus labor in convincing human terms. So I was still looking for a way to see literature in a marxian perspective as both more cognitively penetrating and emotionally satisfying than simply as a series of case-studies in victimization, no matter how moving in themselves some of these (e.g., *The Dollmaker*) might be.

Among Minnesota's bounties were the visiting professors of American literature who came every summer, including one year Robert E. Spiller, editor-in-chief of the forthcoming *Literary History of the United States,* a much heralded project at that time. The topic of Spiller's graduate seminar was "Theories of American Literature," and I persisted by writing my term paper on the existing marxist theories. When it came time to read this paper aloud to the class, at one point I used the phrase "classical marxism," and Spiller stopped me right there. When I looked up, his face was beet red, and he launched into a five-minute tirade about my dignifying marxism with the honorific word "classical." As I remember it, my argument was that the ideological tunnel vision of current marxist theory involved an oversimplification of classical marxism, and, since Spiller evidently could still see this as an attack on marxism, he gave me an A.

6.

Bobby and I are both warm and outgoing people, also big talkers, and our home was a place where friends regularly dropped in and sometimes stayed for dinner on the spur of the moment. Once we had children—Alex on April 4, 1951 and Linda on November 20, 1952—Bobby stopped working and tried to keep writing while caring for the kids. Thanks to the Communist Party, I think we were a gender-enlightened couple by the standards of that time: I shared in the housework, cooking, diapering, and I'd often begin doing my class reading, or writing my term paper, around 10 p.m. But this was not gender equity: I was out of the house most of the day pursuing my vaunted life of the mind in a network of fellow students and teachers, while Bobby was at home with no one to talk to while hoping to read or write while the kids took their naps. She got some stimulation from friends who stopped by, but that wasn't the same thing.

Underlying the gender gap were emerging differences in temperament and neurosis that kept creating the friction which, despite our good will and years of trying, now in Minneapolis and later in Columbus, we never found ways to work through and grow on. Instead, we denied, evaded, papered over; we distracted ourselves with children, friends, renovating old houses, visiting our families in Chicago. In everyday intimate relations I am your classic passive-aggressive, and I was of course certain when we fought that my arguments were logically flawless. When Bobby failed to see how wrong she really was, I would storm out of the house after delivering some choice inflammatory barbs, and during my walk compose in my head a closely reasoned letter explaining once again why I was right. A couple of these letters I actually wrote and delivered.

Bobby is neither passive-aggressive nor logically flawless. She wears her heart and mind on her sleeve, and her sleeve can balloon out to fill the whole room. Our coal-furnace apartment house was a four-plex, and in those days before clothes dryers, the tenants had to agree on weekly wash-days for using the basement clothes-lines. Bobby experienced this as an imposition on her freedom to do the laundry when the spirit moved her. The novel she'd begun writing, whose loving knowledge of life makes you laugh and then cry by the dazzling mimesis of its individual scenes, was criticized over years by friends who read it (including me) for its weakness in overall structure. Following long struggle with this novel after our lives diverged, she found her *métier* in shorter literary forms and in oral performance whose mimicry and timing still bring down the house. Looking back now, I think she was beginning to feel alienated from the academic world where I'd begun to thrive, and also from me as our frictions kept recurring.

But I didn't see it then, nor perhaps did she, and we kept on trying in the same old ways.

7.

I did well in my course-work, wrote two extra-long term papers in lieu of an M.A. thesis, won second prize for distinction in literary studies, and became an over-stimulated teacher of freshman composition. When the law school asked the English department to create an advanced composition course for pre-law students, my law school experience put me in line for the job, and I was put in touch with Professor Terrell, the philosophy department's logician. Together we devised a course that combined expository writing with formal logic, which I then had to learn on the fly when I initiated the course. Luckily, the textbook Terrell chose was Monroe Beardsley's wonderfully accessible *Practical Logic*, and mastering this book was formative for me. It deepened my ability to see the strengths and weaknesses of my own and others' arguments, and also to see the difference between evidence that is truly functional and evidence that is merely "make-weight" in support of those arguments.

The teaching assistants, perhaps even more than the faculty, were regularly courted by publishers' representatives (traveling salesmen) seeking textbook adoptions for the freshman English course that enrolled thousands of students. But one of these who remains for me an American cultural hero had nothing to do with freshman English. Harvey McCaleb was a country boy, maybe six feet three and impeccably dressed in Brooks Brothers suits, whose Oklahoma twang sounded wildly out of place in our ivy-covered halls. He represented Rinehart & Co, an upstart New York publisher established for the sole purpose of keeping in the family all the profits from Mary Roberts Rinehart's best-selling detective novels. Rinehart was evidently indifferent to textbooks until Harvey approached them with a proposal that had been rejected by his previous employer, the legendary Macmillan & Co. The result was the Rinehart Editions that brought the paperback revolution to the college textbook industry.

Until that time, textbooks for English literature courses were expensive hardback anthologies containing more Renaissance poetry or Victorian prose than could possibly be taught, which even so had to be supplemented by still other anthologies or by one of the few Modern Library novels then available. The Rinehart Editions greatly enlarged this variety of novels, and also added manageable collections of essays, poetry, or short stories either by single authors or historical schools. All this enabled teachers to devise more varied and comprehensive course syllabi than before, soon in such fields as history and philosophy as well as the modern literatures, and at far less cost to students. The Rinehart Editions were then swiftly imitated, by Houghton Mifflin with its Riverside Editions, The Modern Library with its College Editions, and Norton with its Critical Editions, in a vast overnight enlargement of student resources for liberal education.

I would never have known Harvey's part in all this if he hadn't once let it slip when we had him over for a home-cooked meal. In his semi-annual trips to Minneapolis, he took care of business with the faculty each morning and then hung out with us graduate students the rest of the day. He was not a big reader but an alert student of the publishing industry, and back in Tulsa he and his wife had four children who would soon be taught in college by our generation of professors. So Harvey was unassumingly open in using us as antennae without having to play the New Yorker in his fancy clothes but just be the home boy he really was.

I also made a small foray of my own into the textbook world, the indirect result of an abrupt change in topic for my Ph.D. dissertation. Henry Smith was now my adviser for a dissertation on Henry James, and I was well into my reading when Smith was appointed literary executor of the Mark Twain Papers at UC-Berkeley. His dissertation students had to scramble for new advisers, none of whom felt comfortable with my topic. One suggested instead a dissertation on William Dean Howells, of whom I'd read enough to know that he offers meager food for thought. So I proposed a couple of alternative topics in American literature, none of which got a sponsor, and then bolted to Shakespeare, on whose Roman plays I had written my term paper for the Shakespeare seminar. Once I began developing this topic with the full support of Professor Leonard Unger, I was invited to edit a collection of articles on *Julius Caesar*, and this early "casebook" became my first publication.

My rejection of Howells for Shakespeare was a defining act in more ways than I knew then. For one thing, it connected once and for all my two interests in aesthetics and politics. William Dean Howells is at first glance an inviting subject for a would-be marxist Ph.D. dissertation. He had risked his celebrity by protesting the execution of anarchists falsely accused of fomenting Chicago's 1886 Haymarket Riot, a landmark event in the American history of class struggle. He had written a utopian novel, *A Traveler From Altruria*, and his realist novel *A Hazard of New Fortunes* is rare for its depiction of a streetcar strike. But Howells's on-and-off sympathy for the working class fails to produce even a clue to class expropriation as a social process, and his fiction is neither artfully engaging nor emotionally moving. Documenting all this might produce an acceptable dissertation, but I also thought it would lead to an intellectual dead end. So what, if still one more novelist moved by the misery produced by capitalism can't go on to imagine this misery's means of production in and through the form of his art?

Shakespeare's Roman plays don't identify class expropriation either, but their powerful drama of political process is full of promise in that regard. Politics is the handmaiden of expropriation, and sooner or later can't be represented without reference to expropriation. Here was at least a starting point, in the work of a writer who is capable of both the intellectual depth and artistic coherence through which expropriation might come to be represented as human experience. The end point came some forty years later, when I was able to analyze Shakespeare's greatest tragedy as fundamentally concerned with the politics and culture of class expropriation.

A second result of my turn to Shakespeare is that it led me to become, at least in one scholarly perspective, a jack-of-all-trades and master of none. To engage Shakespeare seriously, you must certainly learn a lot, yet not everything you might wish, about English Renaissance history and culture, and for me this meant sacrificing the opportunity to learn everything I might wish about American literary history and culture. I've felt embarrassed ever since before colleagues in both fields who have read more than I have, and even now I worry whether I've read all I need to in order to carry off a particular project.

8.

My immediate worry was whether a dissertation on Shakespeare by someone claiming a specialty in American literature would be held against me by prospective employers who could think I was spreading myself too thin. When I started applying for jobs in the autumn of 1955, my mother came to Minneapolis for a week in which she typed thirty application letters in variations tailored to the schools I was applying to. At that time the academic job market was just opening up in response to the post-war growth in university enrollments, and for Minnesota Ph.D's this meant we had a chance at jobs in schools like Kansas State in addition to schools like St. Cloud State. I applied mostly to public universities whose land-grant mission appealed to me politically, but also to a handful of elite four-year colleges whose reputedly eager students appealed to me pedagogically. But with those I was given a quick comeuppance by the president of Sarah Lawrence, a famous liberal whose articles on politics and education regularly appeared in *The Atlantic Monthly* and *The Nation.* The first sentence of Harold Taylor's return-mail response to my letter of application was "Thank you for your letter of____, and for the suggestion that you teach at Sarah Lawrence."

The only nibble my applications brought was for a one-year instructorship at the University of Alberta, with no chance of renewal, and I had to wonder whether my errant dissertation on Shakespeare was killing me on the job market. Then just when I thought I might have to look for other means of livelihood, the chairman at Minnesota got a call from the chairman at Ohio State asking him to recommend someone they might consider for one of their openings. In the previous year Minnesota had hired Murray Krieger from Ohio State, its first ever Big Ten Ph.D., who was soon to have an illustrious career as a   literary theorist. Now Robert Estrich, whose chairmanship at Ohio State was soon to become a legend in our profession, wanted to return the favor.

That was just like him. Bob Estrich grew up pushing a horse-drawn plow on an Appalachian farm in southeast Ohio, and although I never knew him to take regular exercise for the rest of his life, he kept the physique that would make a body-builder envious. His Ph.D. was from Ohio University, as improbable as one could get, and his specialty was Anglo-Saxon and medieval literature. He could read four or five languages, he was steeped in European history, and among the new generation of faculty he was mentoring at Ohio State were two soon-to-become renowned medievalists, Morton Bloomfield and Donald R. Howard (whose Florida Ph.D. was almost as *declasse* as Estrich's.).

The novel on his bed table in the hotel room where he interviewed me at the annual convention of the Modern Language Association was Leopardi's *The Leopard*. We were alone, he was chain-smoking, and his questions on Shakespeare's Roman plays were as informed and probing as his questions on Henry James. By the end of our hour I sensed that, if anything, he found my dissertation on Shakespeare an added attraction to my American literature specialty, and indeed a few weeks later he offered me the job. I accepted immediately, but not without misgivings. Relieved as I was to be offered any job whatever, and drawn as I was to Bob Estrich himself, I'd heard all kinds of horror stories, most of them true, about the hysterical McCarthyism of Columbus, Ohio.

The city's great political icon was US Senator John W. Bricker, a soft-brained reactionary upon whose death the university named its administration building for him. Local banks had big banners on their porticos, and homeowners everywhere had signs on their front lawns, proclaiming a multitude of anti-communist slogans. My teaching contract included a loyalty oath to uphold the Constitution, and within a month of our arrival I was visited at home by a pair of FBI agents, good cop and bad cop with their pincer strategy designed to get me to name names while my children stood gaping. I declined, and meanwhile my friends kept saying, "Ohio State is a great place to move from. Do the publishing that will get you an offer elsewhere, then escape." But when I later got chances to go elsewhere, I decided I didn't need to. Columbus became my home for life, and while I've often wished it was in the mountains or by the sea, the richness of my Ohio State experience has left me with no regrets.

CHAPTER 4: AN ACADEMIC VOCATION:

COLUMBUS, 1956-76

On seven of our first eight Saturdays in Columbus, Bobby and I went to cocktail parties in faculty homes, where the men wore suits and ties, the women cocktail dresses, and the host walked round the living room with a water pitcher in each hand, pouring martinis from one and manhattans from the other while inviting the straight drinkers to make their highballs in the kitchen. Every year now for a decade, the Ohio State English department was hiring four or five new members, and the cocktail party was its way of getting acquainted. The tenured faculty got to meet Bob Estrich's new recruits, we got to meet each other, and everyone got to see who could hold their liquor.

We had all been hired as new Ph.D. Instructors at $4500 a year for 1956-7, on a four-year probationary appointment and a three-quarter teaching load of ten courses. During our first two years, eight of these ten were freshman and advanced writing, and during the quarter each year when I taught four writing courses, I graded 104 student themes every ten days. In my third year the teaching load began to be reduced, soon to five courses a year, and the teaching of freshman English by regular faculty began to be phased out; we were replaced by part-timers as smart as we were in an academic class hierarchy that was soon to define English departments everywhere. We then got to teach for the first time advanced undergraduate courses in our specialties, but no graduate seminars before getting tenure.

Our first offices were bull-pens, two rows five desks deep with an aisle between, and this was upscale compared to the converted classrooms where 70 graduate assistants teaching freshman English shared 35 desks in morning and afternoon shifts.

We Instructors shared our offices with Assistant Instructors, almost all of them faculty wives or single women teaching writing. On the first day of each quarter, the hundreds of students enrolled in freshman English at a given hour were herded like cattle along a basement corridor, where they were counted out in groups of 26 and led by their teacher to a classroom across campus, who knew where? I taught freshman English in a memorabilia room of the football stadium, in various basement classrooms without windows, and—my favorite—in a home economics classroom whose walls were lined with sinks and washing machines.

I also taught off-campus to earn extra money. Bob Estrich regularly got requests for short courses in the evenings, and he distributed these among those of us with young families who didn't have independent incomes. During the four years in which I had to earn promotion and tenure while grading all those themes, I taught six-week classes in grammar and usage to the staff of the Ohio Credit Union League and the Columbus chapter of the National Secretaries Association, along with *Romeo and Juliet* to a high school honors class, all at the standard rate of $25 per session.

During these years also, our marriage came unraveled. The children were now reaching school age, Alex going on six and Linda on four when we arrived in Columbus, and just when we were settled into our new life, with Bobby back to work on her novel and me walking them to school, Alex contracted rheumatic fever and had to be kept home for eighteen months. We all had to adjust—I even took him to stock car races after failing to enchant him with recordings of Mozart—and we bought him a guitar without guessing that in his prime as a social worker he would also be leading a jazz band. Now the brunt of his care fell on Bobby, who managed even so to keep at her writing and get a fellowship to Yaddo, the famous writers' retreat, where she went for two summers, finished a draft of her novel, and began her later publicized affair with Saul Bellow. Both times my mother came from Chicago to help with the kids, and meanwhile Bobby and I entered psychotherapy at a public facility built on to Ohio's red brick insane asylum.

I also reached for support to the Judaism I'd grown up in and then drifted away from. My grandparents on both sides were Orthodox, and my liberal parents, who were no longer believers, honored their parents by keeping kosher, observing the Jewish holidays with their powerful rituals and wonderful food, sending Chuck and me to Hebrew school until we were Bar Mitzvahed, and explaining how they wanted to expose us to the Jewish tradition so that we could then make an informed choice whether to adopt it for ourselves.

At one point I could read the Old Testament comfortably in Hebrew, but now I couldn't find in it any help for my pain. I joined with other new Jewish faculty in establishing a congregation of our own, Beth Tikvah, and in our first home at the university's Hillel Foundation we men took turns as rabbi in conducting Friday night services while also teaching our children in Sunday School. When I was growing up, the opening of the Ark and reading of the Torah had often filled my heart with a mystical feeling of connection with God and my people. But my new synagogue activity did not lead me to recover that sense of connection, and meanwhile, my reading of Jewish theologians like Martin Buber and Abraham Heschel did more to confirm my secular humanism than my ancestors' faith and practice.

I was thus a timely candidate for psychotherapy, and here I was lucky in being assigned to a gifted Gestalt therapist and student of the great Fritz Perls, Vincent O'Connell, whose family Catholicism, I was soon to discover, had also failed him at a decisive moment in life. My later therapy experiences taught me that while no single approach has a monopoly on effectiveness, Gestalt works best for me. Perls wrote that "…most psychotherapies are trying to get to the deepest depth. We are trying to get to the outermost surface," and O'Connell wrote of a life crisis like mine as an "organismic event"—emotional, intellectual, and behavioral—that challenges one's habitual way of engaging others, which in my case prominently involved "the hypnosis of the spoken word." In supporting me through the fear of breaking this hypnosis by talking less and listening more, O'Connell shared his own uncertainties in a manner that made him more like a teacher, and his practice of therapy was later to have a huge impact on my practice in the classroom.

It also helped me right then to engage with Bobby. We both listened harder and were able to change for a time some deeply rooted behaviors. But we had a lot of ground to make up, and I think this was harder for her in her distracted self-absorption than it was for me. At one stage, it felt to me for a couple of months as if we were renewing our union, but then we couldn't sustain this, and in 1960 she asked me to move out. When we divorced a year later, my brother Chuck came down to arrange the legal details, and both our therapists urged me not to contest custody of the children because they were the "life-line" that kept Bobby grounded. This was a relief to me because I shunned that responsibility. Bobby got a secretarial job in Ohio State's psychology department, I saw the kids twice a week and took them on vacations, and then in 1962, a year after I got tenure, she moved with them to San Francisco.

I don't think it registered with me at the time what this really meant for my relationship with my children. It was one thing not to contest for custody, and something else to be 2000 miles away during their formative years. But in those days I romanticized my ability to overcome all obstacles, and I also thought Bobby had a better chance with the children in a city more congenial to single mothers than Columbus back then. I wrote Alex and Linda letters, I phoned them, and took them on summer vacations. I wrote a letter of protest to Alex's junior high principal when he was the first boy in his school to grow shoulder-length hair (in San Francisco!), got attacked by his classmates, and was told by the principal that the problem was his. But none of this really overcame our physical distance, and in my isolation I threw myself all the more into my work, making my students and colleagues a substitute family. This was deeply congenial to my socialism, but it also confirmed my disconnect from my children.

What with grading those themes, moonlighting in the evenings, going through a divorce, and trying to earn tenure and promotion in four years, my memory of these years is mostly a blur. I was mostly just trying to survive, and it was no surprise that when I came up for promotion in 1960, I had no actual publications but only a couple of article manuscripts for my senior colleagues to read. They read them, and on the evening before my appointment with Bob Estrich to hear their decision, Bobby and I were taken out to what seemed a celebratory dinner by two senior professors with their wives, one of them Bill Charvat, my sponsor in American literature. In those days there was no formal evaluation of teaching, and during the previous year Charvat had asked me to take over for a day his class in American Literary Realism. "I'm all burned out teaching Dreiser," he said, "and I'm hoping you can breathe some fresh life into him." I spent two weeks preparing for this one hour, and my performance evidently satisfied him about my teaching while also getting me started to write my article on Dreiser.

But that article was not yet accepted for publication on the morning of my appointment with Estrich, and neither was the one on tragic form in *Macbeth* which had begun life as a term paper for Allen Tate at Minnesota. So Estrich's message was not quite what I was expecting after last night's fancy dinner: the decision on my tenure was postponed for a year. But I could at least see the dinner as an act of faith, and to everyone's relief a year later, this faith was rewarded. The Dreiser article was published in 1961, then reprinted five times over forty years, and the *Macbeth* article, also published in 1961 by *The Shakespeare Quarterly*, brought me an elite invitation to contribute to that journal's special issue in honor of Shakespeare's 400th birthday.

This story of my first promotion was not unusual in those years, and it must sound like a fairy tale in today's corporate university. Not only were two good articles deemed sufficient to earn tenure, but the peer community of one's colleagues was deemed competent to judge them. True, as Estrich then sardonically told me, a couple of these colleagues had reservations about my age: since I was now all of 35, my publishing career would be seriously foreshortened. But as he also told me, this reservation did not affect either their judgment of my work or their confidence in judging it. Literary scholarship was then being pursued as a holistic discipline that everyone now saw must be enlarged in scope, but only through a further division of labor that didn't keep us from being qualified readers of each other's work.

In today's university this enlargement of scope has occurred, and the intellectual range of today's literary and cultural scholarship dwarfs that of the profession I first entered. Yet like so many expansions of market production—tomato growing, toilet making, book publishing—our broadened scholarship has come at a price in commodity fetishism. Nowadays one must not only have a book in print to earn the first promotion, but this ostentatious production is then also subject to ostentatious evaluation. In my department, the candidate's book must be sent to six outside evaluators, half again as many as can be functional, and, among other requirements, its author must submit a list of footnote citations to this book by every Tom, Dick, and Harry. A scholar with a story like mine could never earn tenure now.

2.

My professional life thus began, for all practical purposes, only after I was awarded tenure, and I believe I got even to this starting line only because of (besides Vincent O'Connell) my excitement and confusion at the vista opening before me. I was being paid and protected to do two things I now knew I loved doing, cultivating my mind in trying to understand human life as revealed by the literary imagination, and inseparably in this process cultivating also the minds of my students. In high school I'd acquired my first full-sized bicycle by borrowing the $22 from my father and repaying him with my tips as a Western Union messenger in a red light district. I'd been a lifeguard and a bellhop, I'd wired jukeboxes, and in university I'd graduated to grilling ham & eggs and slicing lox. What with all that plus the 84th Field Hospital, I'd seen enough to know that I was as lucky (almost) to have landed here as to have come home from the war.

None of which meant that I also knew how to do what I was now doing, and that was the big excitement. Then as now, a college professor was expected to become proficient in the three areas of teaching, scholarship, and service. But few of us are capable of an equal fit in all three, and in each case the only way to find out was by trying. As if that weren't already heady enough, the academic world was just then opening to its great sea change of the 60s and 70s, and, in adapting ourselves to the system during those decades, we also had a rare chance to adapt the system to our individual strengths and sense of purpose. We had the opportunity to find a personal vocation, and that is how I spent the next fifteen years.

Teaching, scholarship, and service remain for some people parallel activities, while for others they come to permeate each other. Some who become fine scholars remain only passable teachers, and some fine teachers only passable scholars. Some ripen as scholars only after they've done so as teachers (or vice versa), others do less scholarship over time and devote themselves to service, and still others merge all three so that it is hard to see where one leaves off and another begins. My friend Marlene Longenecker was an early winner of the university's distinguished teaching award who published very little. But her graduate students regularly won the department's annual prizes for best term paper, M.A. thesis, or Ph.D. dissertation, and one went on to win a Pulitzer Prize. Meanwhile, Marlene's service in helping establish our Women's Studies Program, and then as Chair of Women's Studies during its fragile formative years, led to her appointment as press secretary to the Ohio governor's wife, for which she took a leave of absence and then returned to the university and won another teaching award. As things worked out in ways she could not have foreseen, her teaching, scholarship, and service became all of a piece over a thirty-year career.

I had no idea how things might work out for me, but by temperament and inclination I became first and foremost a teacher, and my evolving sense of purpose as a teacher made a fortunate fit with the 1960s student rebellion against the remoteness and rigidity of their professors. In that decade of national upheaval, the civil rights movement, anti-Vietnam War movement, New Age movement, and feminist movement (to name only those) converged in a broadside attack on the white American Establishment with its gray flannel infrastructure—the government and political parties; Wall St. and the military-industrial complex; the churches and universities; the ticky-tacky suburbs where the baby boom rebels had grown up. All the new movements reached into the universities, and two had the long-term effect of re-shaping our scholarship and curriculum with the establishment of Black Studies and Women's Studies programs in the 1970s. Meanwhile, they all challenged us immediately as teachers to become more accessible, flexible, and transparent, and our classrooms were soon changing in a manner to encourage the kind of teaching I was learning to do.

By a kind of osmosis, as I remember it, somewhere around 1964 college professors stopped smoking pipes, wearing ties and jackets to class, and carrying leather briefcases. We all adopted variations of the hitherto exclusive "Harvard book bag," a forest green canvas bag thrown casually over one shoulder to show that you could belong to the *demos* of American democracy even if you did have a Harvard Ph.D.. In the few classrooms whose chairs were not bolted to the floor, we began arranging them in circles instead of rows, with no front or back for the students and no place of power for the teacher. And if the class was small enough, we began meeting it in our homes.

But if with all this you were still going to lecture, or only to ask "Guess what I'm thinking?", then your style of tobacco, dress, book bag, or classroom could loosen things up only so far. As our students were soon saying, you were still keeping all the power to yourself, which is exactly what I insisted on doing when I first got to teach the literature I loved. I took to the traditional classroom like a duck to water, and in the intoxication of teaching my first literature courses, I forgot all about Edward Levi, William Rea Keast, and Vincent O'Connell. I lectured every day, and the hour was never long enough for what I absolutely had to say. Preparing lectures forced me to think more deeply into the subject so as to organize my analysis in a coherent progression. It also enabled me to hog the limelight, which may sound like vanity, and some of it surely was. But I think the satisfaction I most wanted was not applause for my performance but acceptance for my ideas, and the other side of that coin was my grandiose faith that my ideas could change the world. I became even so a competent lecturer, although a far cry from Samuel Monk while interrupting myself to ask "Am I clear?" as I kept thinking out loud. (Once or twice when I saw I couldn't be clear because I hadn't been able in fact to think the issue through, I dismissed the class and said I'd try to do better tomorrow.) And then over time, as I began repeating the same lectures with no longer much feeling of personal growth, I remembered Vincent O'Connell and found ways to start listening.

In this I was also influenced by two thinkers I'd been reading, the Jewish theologian Martin Buber and my old Chicago teacher J.V. Cunningham. O'Connell in fact had urged me to read Buber, whose version of Judaism as an "I and Thou" relationship had a lot in common with the relationship he was cultivating with me. Buber claims with rare eloquence that the sacred is immanent in everyday experience—in those encounters, whether between two people or between a person and a tree, in which we open ourselves to the otherness of the Other in the unique specificity of its individual life. Cunningham made a similar claim for the study of literature in his book *Woe or Wonder: The Emotional Effect* of *Shakespearean Tragedy*, where he decried the practice of reading our meanings into words that meant something else to Shakespeare in his otherness: when Edgar in *King Lear* famously says that "Ripeness is all," we read this "ripeness" to mean "maturity of experience," whereas to Shakespeare it meant just the opposite, that "the fruit will fall in its time" whether or not we have attained maturity of experience. "The problem...here raised with respect to literature," wrote Cunningham, "is really the problem of any human relationship: Shall we understand another on his terms or on ours?"

I was now able to see that this problem involves not only the relationship I wanted my students to have with Shakespeare but also a relationship I wanted to have with them. I knew how I had grown intellectually by talking back silently to Shakespeare in my teaching and writing, and this problem-solving growth is what the land-grant university aims above all to produce in its students. So instead of expecting my students just to keep on listening, or else to read my mind, I began struggling for the patience to read theirs as they struggled to become articulate. And as it turned out, for the next thirty years the most frequent praise I was to hear for my teaching, from sophomores through Ph.D. students, was that I took with total seriousness their most stupid, befuddled, or non-responsive answers to my questions (also the bizarre questions they sometimes asked), and asked them follow-up questions which, in the root meaning of the word "educate," drew them out instead of stuffing me in. I learned to honor their minds, and, if the discussion did become productive, I also called attention to how their ideas were building on each other's, so that any feeling of accomplishment we came out with was one in which all could share.

I remember two undergraduate courses where I cut my teeth in doing this, a 1960s honors seminar in the novels of Dostoevsky and a 1970s version of the American Realism course in which Bill Charvat had given me my big chance. The Dostoevsky was new to me, which meant that I didn't have all the answers beforehand but would be substantially conducting my education in public. (A professor of Slavic protested when he heard about it later.) Yet this also meant that my great temptation was to overwhelm the students with my giddy response to the great Dostoevskian interplay of idea and form. So I zipped up my lip in class and wrote down this response at home, in a cumulative letter to the students that I distributed only at the end as a personal summing up. This freed me not only to conduct the class entirely by question-and-answer, but also to avoid policing the discussion, Keast-like, with questions leading only to what my letter would tell them anyway. Not only did they arrive on their own at 93% of what I was writing in my letter, but their departures from my erstwhile agenda produced ideas as deep as mine that had not occurred to me. The more I came to trust them as we progressed, the more relaxed I became in expecting them to see what I saw, and then some, if my questions just kept them focused on the issue at hand. It was a virtuous circle.

These were of course select honors students, yet still and all land-grant students whose ragged blue jeans were a badge of income and not fashion, and who needed the support and confidence to depend on their own intelligence. Once they started doing that, there was no stopping them, and they inspired me to keep moving in this direction. From one point of view, this kind of teaching is hugely inefficient and wasteful: what you might (or might not) lead the students to figure out for themselves in an hour, you could have told them directly in ten minutes. But what you told them could also be forgotten in five after they walked out the door, whereas thinking out the problem for themselves was something they could grow on. This was for me a new way of engaging both the subject and the students, in a process that was applicable far beyond the works of Dostoevsky.

I didn't go on to teach every class in this fashion, but I kept doing it regularly, and on one memorable occasion changed places with my students. In the American Realism course, I tried what for me was the risky experiment of allowing Kate Chopin's *The Awakening* to become an assigned reading. This long-forgotten novel was then being recovered by second-wave feminists whose work I admired, and I was in the awkward position of regarding it as aesthetically insubstantial, more like a scenario than a finished work of art, and not really fit company in this course for such white male masterpieces as *Huckleberry Finn, The Portrait of a Lady,* or *Sister Carrie.* Much as I wanted to keep an open mind, when our week on *The Awakening* arrived, I still couldn't see a way even to introduce this novel without revealing my condescension. So I walked into that room of 45 people, slid into a chair in the middle of the fourth row, and remained straight-faced and silent in response to their expectant looks. After an anxious five minutes, they saw it was up to them, and the first to speak were two white males, both good students, who said they'd been bowled over by *The Awakening.* They couldn't wait to explain why, they were challenged by women who thought they'd gone berserk, and for the next hour that class was like a revival meeting. By the end they didn't need me, but I couldn't tolerate that and came forward to connect the strands of their now thorough analysis. Meanwhile, that hour made me a convert (of sorts) to *The Awakening.* It may not have measured up to my standard for supreme works of art, but its feminist narrative was intellectually enlightening and emotionally moving to some very thoughtful people, and that was something I had to learn to respect.

These classroom experiences were formative for me, and they gave me a measure of socialist satisfaction beyond anything I was to find in my political activity outside the classroom. In the participatory democracy we socialists dream of, not all participants will be equally informed, analytical, articulate, or caring. Some who are less forthcoming will be deeper of mind or more generous of spirit than some who speak first or best, and the community will need everyone's personal growth and collective wisdom in lending their ears. It will certainly need leaders who can ask the right questions and then listen hard, in a classroom that works for them as for everyone else.

3.

As I grew into my authority and poise as a teacher, I also became a protagonist of teaching in my department, and this occurred in tandem with events surrounding Ohio State's 1970 student strike that led many of us to re-think yet again the purpose of American higher education. Bob Estrich retired from the chairmanship in 1964 and was succeeded by Al Kuhn, with me as vice-chair. During five years in this position, I was involved in every aspect of the department's activity, and when in 1968 it took the revolutionary step of appointing a committee on teaching, I was named chair of this committee. At Ohio State until that time, a man's classroom was his castle, and observing him teach was an invasion of his privacy. But we had begun to acknowledge that teaching, like scholarship, is an acquired skill, that it is a form of publication also like scholarship, and that it can be evaluated and rewarded with as much (or as little) confidence as we are actually capable of with scholarship. Our committee recommended that all faculty teaching be evaluated both by students and colleagues, that we hold training sessions for graduate assistants teaching for the first time, and that tenured faculty begin teaching freshman English again. These recommendations were implemented over time, and all that failed to materialize was for the rewards of teaching to become commensurate with those of scholarship.

During the two years following this committee's recommendations, 1968-70, both the nation and the campus were shaken by events that culminated at Ohio State in the 1970 strike that shut down the university for two weeks, after which it re-opened with the campus cordoned off by 5000 members of the Ohio National Guard armed with tear gas, rifles, and bayonets. This strike materialized in a convergence of the civil rights and anti-war movements, and its initial demands, presented by perhaps 200 students (among 40,000 then on campus) gathered on the steps of the administration building, were the appointment of a university vice-president for black student affairs and the cessation of war research and military recruiting on campus. The university's halting and equivocal response to these demands produced a campus-wide explosion: within a week the strike attracted thousands of students and resulted in the calling out of the National Guard, 600+ arrests, and an estimated cost of $1,500,000. The strike leaders were overwhelmed by the turnout, and it was clear that they had tapped into long-standing student resentments, reaching far beyond affirmative action and the Vietnam War, that they had not been aware of.

The faculty's devotion to teaching was not a strike issue, yet one resentment that quickly found a voice was the university's indifference to undergraduate education. The dean of one college was known to have instructed his curriculum committee to reject all proposals for new undergraduate courses, and over the three academic quarters of the strike year, 1969-70, undergraduates had been closed out of 1200 courses for which they tried to register. As I remember the daily noon-hour speeches on the Oval, the closed course issue became a key motive for the mass of students who flocked to the strike. (Two faculty members wrote a history of the strike while it was still fresh in memory, of which the university library's copies were promptly "disappeared," and my account here draws upon my personal copy.)

I was of course a participant, along with many faculty, in many kinds of support for the strikers, which on one sunny afternoon involved our forming a line in the space between them and the National Guard's bared bayonets. But well beyond our day-by-day involvement, even we leftists were shaken by the breadth and depth of the students' frustration with the entire university. That clearly included us, and following the strike in the summer of 1970, I had some long talks with two colleagues, my friend Gordon Grigsby and my new wife Joan Webber, about changing our entire manner of teaching. Then we three informed Al Kuhn that we would be conducting a new experiment in our autumn classes and would write reports on this experiment for our colleagues to see.

On the first day of class that autumn, each of us distributed the customary course syllabus listing authors to be studied and works to be read, the days of lecture and discussion sessions, plus a writing requirement, and we explained to the students that they were free to take the course in this traditional format. But then we also explained that they were free to modify this format to suit their personal interests, aversions, and preferred ways of learning. In my American Renaissance course, for example, *The Scarlet Letter* and *Moby-Dick* were both listed readings. But if you felt suffocated for the moment by *The Scarlet Letter* from previous high school or college courses, you could skip it here and read *Moby-Dick* more lovingly, or some Hawthorne short stories that were not on the syllabus, or Whitman's complete *Leaves of Grass* and nothing else. If you found lectures a waste of time as compared with class discussion or individual tutorials, you could skip the lectures and attend only the discussions, or take the entire course as a tutorial. And if at this moment in your life the prospect of writing still more three-page analytical papers looked as unproductive as reading *The Scarlet Letter* yet again, you could keep a journal, write a research paper, paint a picture, or compose a song. There would be no examinations, and the course grade would be determined in a teacher-student conference where the student had the last word.

Our aim was to free both the students and ourselves from a production-line mentality where everyone must jump through the same hoops in order to become publicly certified without also becoming personally educated. We wanted to give them both more freedom and more responsibility by respecting from the outset both their minds and their ethics—to draw them here and now into becoming land grant citizens. Their course evaluations afterwards were mostly favorable, and so were our self-evaluations to show our colleagues. These provoked a thoughtful reaction, and I've kept all these years both the student evaluations and the baker's dozen of responses written by colleagues in advance of the department meeting where our experiment was debated.

What rocked the boat most for some colleagues was letting the students grade themselves. As these people put it, that compromised the integrity of the grading system and cheapened the value of the B.A. degree. But it turned out in this regard that we had put our finger on a problem the university soon came to recognize: at Ohio State as elsewhere, the "pass/fail" grade option became widespread in the 70s. It also turned out that our students thought the chance to grade themselves was the least attractive feature of the experiment. Their enthusiasm was for the flexibility of readings, assignments, and classroom relations with which we were trying to cultivate their individual sense of purpose.

Yet several students I'd had in previous classes wrote in their evaluations of this one that I was a teacher who didn't need these anarchist procedures to cultivate their intellectual independence. I'd been doing that already, they said, and I also now saw that the flexibility I was offering involved a costly trade-off. When different members of the class are reading somewhat different texts and attending different class or tutorial sessions, the opportunity to cultivate the collective problem-solving of those Dostoevsky and American Realism classes was substantially diminished.

Our flexibility was also highly labor-intensive, and over the following years a number of colleagues joined us in trying to modify the original conception without sacrificing its purpose and spirit. People recognized something useful in what we had attempted, and while the 70s transformation of American higher education surely would have transpired without us, our effort to think globally and act locally made a difference in our community.

4.

Over these years of devotion to teaching, I remained sporadic, diffuse, and still groping as a scholar. The little work I published earned respect, but it did not acquire the critical mass, momentum, and trajectory that I came to envy in others, beginning with Don Howard, a shining model of the scholar's vocation who had come to Ohio State the year before I did. Don lived in our neighborhood, often dropped in to gossip with me and Bobby on his way home from the university, and sometimes stayed for supper. When the English department got a new building in 1960, he and I picked out an office to share from the architect's blueprint, and for the next two years before he moved on, Don's scholarly work, along with his conversation about the academic profession and the life of the mind, set a standard to which I was then to hold myself and all others.

Like Allen Tate and Meridel LeSueur, Donald R. Howard was an outsize personality who you remember for the rest of your life. His life, as he often said, was a constant oscillation between the pleasures of the flesh and what his medieval Christianity called "the contempt of the world." He was witty and urbane, he loved fine clothes, his cocktail was the Rob Roy, and he was notoriously short-tempered. Back in the 1950s, no men's store in Columbus carried Brooks Brothers clothes, and a Brooks salesman came to town twice a year to take orders. Don was first on his list, and once his wardrobe was filled out to his liking, he traded in his Chevrolet for a Mercedes sport coupe. Years later, after he'd moved from

Johns Hopkins to an endowed chair at Stanford, he took me to dinner at a premier San Francisco restaurant. I've forgotten his *entree*, but he was unhappy with the baked potato, and the server took that one back and brought another. But where the first had been underdone, the second was overdone, and Don sent those potatoes back four times, his voice rising each time while the *maitre d'* tried to calm him. By now people were staring at us, but for Don it was the principle of the thing: in a restaurant this pricey they should be able to bake a potato to perfection.

His other side was his monastic discipline in producing a lasting body of exceptional scholarship on medieval literature and culture. He had been raised an Episcopalian and before going to graduate school had served a novitiate in a monastery. Now his whole existence, including the wardrobe and Mercedes, was appended to his scholarly work, which became stunningly versatile, comprehensive, eloquent, and deep. Medievalists are of course famous for their immediate breadth of learning; they have to be comfortable in three or four languages, and in history, theology, and paleography just to get started on their work. But Don Howard was besides all that a serious and imaginative *thinker*, as many knowing readers of his work have testified, and in this respect he exemplified for me a lot of what I'd admired in my teacher Henry Smith.

I was soon to have other colleagues who were this same kind of scholar-thinker—Joan Webber, Jim Kincaid, who became a friend for life, and Tom Mitchell, who, in addition to his own work, became for our profession a rare midwife to thought as editor of *Critical Inquiry*. I felt just as smart as they were, but I couldn't get my work focused they way they did, and my frustration in finding an adequate marxism was only one part of that. Two other parts were my aestheticism and my malingering.

Having declined to write a Ph.D. dissertation on the lukewarm socialist William Dean Howells because he was aesthetically boring, I couldn't resist the red hot anti-socialist Dostoevsky because he was aesthetically compelling. In the long run, of course, submitting your socialism to the challenge of an art as deep as Dostoevsky's can only strengthen or else destroy it. But that was the farthest thing from my mind back then. I was just going where I thought the action was, aesthetic and philosophical—to Shakespeare and Dostoevsky, Balzac and Nietzsche, Melville and James, Kafka and Faulkner (never Joyce or Proust). I turned my Ph.D. dissertation into a book on Shakespeare's philosophical development whose grandiose aim required me to eliminate half of what I'd written and add new material (some of it better than other), including a few pages on *King Lear* that contained in embryo the marxian analysis I was later to develop. This earned me promotion to professor and got me a fellowship to begin a book on Herman Melville, which I then worked at sporadically for twenty-five years before it was published. Here my starting point was Shakespeare's well documented influence on Melville, which I enlarged into an analysis of *Moby-Dick*'s debt to *King Lear* as a historic progression in the capitalist ideology of society and identity.

In writing these books, I tested my ideas in the classroom and refined them in response to the give-and-take with my students. My teaching and scholarship fed each other, until I reached a point much later when revising on the computer became a talking-to-myself as if with my students. Along the way I published a half-dozen articles, accumulated rejections slips, aborted grandiose projects ("The Shared Imagination of Science and Poetry"; "The Disappearance of God on the Road to Socialism in *The Brothers Karamazov*"), and then in retirement published more and better than I'd done the previous thirty years. There was a saying back then that scientists do their best work when they're young and humanists do theirs when they're old, and now I believe that applies to me.

While I was darting hither and yon as a low productivity scholar, my eyes were also being opened to the pretensions and politics of academic scholarship, and for a while this gave me a sour grapes excuse for my malingering. When our beloved Bill Charvat was dying of cancer, I sat at his bedside holding his glass of bourbon for him to sip through a straw, and then, in going through his papers afterwards, discovered that he'd been a consultant to Harvard in filling its vacant professorship left by the death of the legendary F.O. Matthiessen. Harvard spent years trying to fill this vacancy, and it was a revelation to me to see in Charvat's file that when people like Henry Smith turned them down, they suddenly found new merit in candidates they had previously disdained.

I was also learning the blind spots of the outside evaluators to whom we were now required to submit the work of our candidates for promotion. These eminent people could mistake a good book because it threatened their scholarly turf, or because it wasn't the book they wanted written on this subject, or because it lagged behind what two celebrities had proclaimed as the cutting edge of scholarship, or because they were too self-infatuated to see what it was really saying. Such people were the exception, but, like that Harvard search committee, they became for me a continuing reminder how the commoditization of scholarship can produce alienation even among those devoted to the life of the mind.

5.

Joan Webber was one of Bob Estrich's last hires. She had come to Ohio State on a temporary appointment with an unfinished Ph.D. dissertation on the prose style of John Donne, which Estrich must have recognized for the gem it was becoming. When it was finished, he got her a tenure-track appointment, and when it was published as a book, *Contrary Music*, it won Phi Beta Kappa's 1963 Christian Gauss Prize for the year's best work of literary scholarship. I'd helped her find an apartment when she came, and after Bobby and I separated we began seeing each other. I was having a hard time being single and needing to be needed, she was forthcoming with my children, and we shared deep interests in politics and scholarship. We were married in 1962, and the night before the wedding our parents, siblings, and children gathered round my brother Chuck with his guitar and sang a lot of left-wing folk songs we found we had in common. Joan also wanted a child of her own, and our Rachel was born on Halloween in 1964.

Joan's new fame brought her invitations to teach summer sessions at the universities of New Mexico and Colorado, and an offshoot of that was our becoming mountain climbers. We joined the local climbing clubs in Albuquerque and Boulder and later bought a house in Boulder, which we rented out for the school year and returned to in the summers to climb once in mid-week, once on the weekend, and the rest of the time write our articles and prepare our next year's classes. It was in Boulder the summer

Gordon Grigsby came to visit that we three hatched our teaching experiment.

In climbing as in scholarship, Joan was a daring achiever and I a sour malingerer. She had inherited her father's iron constitution, and I my father's cardiovascular frailty along with my mother's depression. High mountains have no mercy, and when we'd reach one "false summit" after another on the way up, she would quicken her pace each time with renewed expectation, while I fell further behind in deepening resentment—at the mountain, at her, at myself. People climb for different reasons, and it took me a while to find mine. Once I stopped trying to keep up and found my own rhythm, I felt a pantheistic surge in connecting with the mountain in its indifference to the life struggling upwards in the great silence above tree line—scraggly mosses, foraging marmots, bristle-cone pines pushing through rock and snow only to hug the ground and avoid the fierce winds. As we socialists must keep reminding ourselves, hope never dies.

Joan later wrote a poem celebrating those pines, yet she experienced climbing differently than I did. Where I was at heart just a hiker whose rhythm could sometimes connect me with the mountain, she came to speak of playing chess with the mountain. On one outing, our mountain club party was to climb Mount Wilson, one of Colorado's famed "fourteeners," which is connected to another, Wilson Peak, by a knife-edged ridge three-quarters of a mile long. We got to the Mount Wilson summit in the sunshine before noon, when the weather can come in and you should be on your way down, and she asked the leader if we could now attempt the traverse to Wilson Peak. He polled the group, half of whom had had enough and turned back. I'd done well and was ready to go on, but soon after we started the weather overtook us, dense clouds that closed down visibility and soaked that ridge in moisture. All we could see was the slimy ledge we were holding onto in our three-point stance while deciding which leg or arm to reach out for the next available hold. It took us more than four hours to go that three-fourths of a mile, and next day we discovered that the sheer drop-off below had been more hundreds of feet than we'd have wanted to contemplate.

Back in Columbus, Joan wrote a second book, and I built a room in the basement for visiting family. I also built from a kit an acoustically spectacular enclosure for my bass-reflex loudspeaker. In this heyday of the LP record, lovers of classical music had a rare opportunity: for the price of a ticket to a live performance you could buy two or three records, with their wonderfully artful jackets, for repeated listening at home. I'd also learned how much musical meaning can be discovered by comparing different performances of the same work, especially those by Beethoven and Tchaikovsky that invite the distorted inflections and tempos with which performers often override the composer. The manager of our Discount Records showed me alternative performances, and he introduced me to composers like Monteverdi, Respighi, and Walton whom I might not have discovered otherwise. Above all, he got me listening more attentively to Berlioz and Stravinsky, for which I now remain grateful every week of the year.

We invited students to our house, and during the strike and years following held our seminars there. Some showed their gratitude by bringing gifts of marijuana, along with their music to play at their volume on my snazzy equipment—the Beatles and Rolling Stones, Bob Dylan and the Grateful Dead, the Moody Blues and the Loving Spoonful. And when my older children came to visit, they introduced us to any number of Joan Baezs, Commander Codys, Linda Ronstadts, and Bob Marleys. I became a fan of the Rolling Stones and George Harrison, and my son Alex began his long-suffering effort to educate me in the wonders of jazz.

We declined the students' dope, but we did try marijuana with our new generation of colleagues for whom it was everyday fare. We also tried for a month with another faculty couple what was then called "open marriage" (aka spouse-sharing) and that led to our breakup. I have felt more pain and guilt over this one experience than any other in my life, and I doubt I can be transparent in trying to tell of it. We four did this in the same spirit as our teaching experiment, with a hope of enlarging our lives by reaching beyond traditional institutions and practices we had long taken for granted. We didn't feel vulnerable in our separate marriages, but we soon discovered otherwise, and both marriages came apart in the aftermath. For one thing, the two alternate couples were not equally connective with one another, and that was just one way the boundaries we were trying to break were more resistant than those we were breaking in the classroom. Once we were no longer bound exclusively, repressed feelings came to the surface and stalled the endeavor, which then required more patience than any of us was prepared for.

I think I'd begun to feel caught between supporting Joan in her burgeoning career, something I needed as much as she did, and resenting her for having a career I didn't have. I think she'd begun feeling caught between a dependence on me and the new confidence that came with her professional accomplishment and surging feminism. We tried marriage counseling, which didn't help, and, now with Joan as before with Bobby, long after the handwriting was on the wall I avoided responsibility for taking the first step and waited for her to kick me out. That way that I could give the appearance to myself of being the one who was wronged.

We kept trying even so, and after she moved with Rachel to the University of Washington in 1972, we re-united in Boulder for a summer in the hope of developing a commuter marriage rather than accept an irrevocable rupture. I went into therapy again, where I was told that my problem originated in my need to placate my mother, and this led to a couple of outbursts at my dear mother that I wish I could take back. Then in the summer of 1974 I took Rachel for two months to the Pellin Institute in Italy, where I attended lecture and group therapy sessions with the gestalt therapist Peter Fleming, whose "Contribution Training" involves a conception of human hurt, and of healing through purpose, that transcends the oedipal dynamics of mother and son.

The Institute operated as a co-op where we took turns with the cooking and housework, and where Rachel got a lot of affectionate day care. I got no immediate help with my marriage, but Peter Fleming's teaching became even so transformative for me. First and best, it made me a viable candidate for a long and fulfilling marriage with Robin. (When Peter later met Robin while we were courting, he told me, "I won't tell you who to marry, but I can tell you that Robin doesn't need anything from you."). It also made me a more alert listener, to a point where I could accomplish the goals of our 1970 experiment with less pedagogical heavy lifting. And in a hundred small ways that made a whole greater than the sum of its parts, Peter Fleming's teaching enlarged my finger-tip effectiveness in the professional arena of service, where I transposed my classroom skills while becoming an effective negotiator, first as department chairman and then as university elder statesman and community activist.

6.

In my first years at Ohio State, what the university called service was limited to two kinds of activity: your work on department, college, and university committees, and any professionally related volunteer work you might be doing in the university or community—as, for example, faculty adviser to a student organization or guest speaker at a community reading group. But as the 60s unfolded, service came to include a wider spectrum of activity, both on campus and off, some of which contributed to the great 70s upheaval, and in this kind of service I was numerous.

Soon after being awarded tenure in 1961, I began my Ohio State career of political activism by proposing revolutionary change in the structure and process of English department government. Our governing body was then the "Senior Staff," consisting of perhaps a dozen-and-a-half full and associate professors, and excluding perhaps ten dozen assistant professors, instructors, assistant instructors, lecturers, and graduate teaching assistants. The Senior Staff met twice a month for lunch at a long table in the Faculty Club, where Bob Estrich sat at the head and transmitted the university administration's latest directives, along with the latest rumors about the legislature's budget mood, the forthcoming deanship vacancy, and the construction schedule for our new building. It appointed the departmental committees and reserved to itself the power to approve of committee proposals.

I don't remember now the contents of a two-page, single-spaced letter, criticizing this system and proposing to replace it with department-wide representative government that I put in everyone's mailbox. Nor do I want to, because I'm sure it was rife with the passive-aggressive sarcasm that I resorted to in those days as a way of showing off. Even so, the response to my proposal was out of all proportion to what I had written. As Don Howard and I were sitting in our new office the afternoon after my missive appeared in faculty mailboxes, first one and then a second Senior Staff member stormed into the office and angrily accused me of destroying the harmony that had kept us working together for years so exceptionally well. They were right about that, but, as Bob Estrich and other seniors also recognized, it was time for this harmony to embrace more people, and the kind of change I proposed was set in motion.

The angry response to my proposal came from those in denial of changes in our department, university, and profession that made this proposal in fact modest. Not only was the lunch table incapable of becoming longer, but it never did serve as a forum for serious deliberation. Far more important was the changing demography and politics of the post-war faculty. We were growing more numerous, hairy, and faintly Jewish just when McCarthyism was giving way to the new movements, and our first big fight, over the university's 1962 "speakers' rule" that was still a relic of McCarthyism, began a decade of agitation and suppression that culminated in the 1970 strike.

By the early 60s Ohio State had an informal network of younger faculty from many departments whose political intensity (which was by no means always radical) went hand in glove with our interdisciplinary interests in history, literature, political theory, and law. We lectured in each other's classes, we jointly advised theses and dissertations, we drank beer at Larry's on Friday afternoons, and we sometimes debated publicly. I once had a go with the political theorist Harry Jaffa, a disciple of Chicago's legendary conservative, Leo Strauss, on the political implications of *Hamlet* and *King Lear*.

In this intellectual climate, even people like Harry Jaffa were upset by a rule that required prior approval by the university administration of anybody invited to speak on campus. Among recent guest speakers invited by student organizations were two or three whom the McCarthyites accused of being communist fellow-travelers, and the Columbus *Dispatch*, a political bastion of Neanderthal conservatism, had called on the university to assume its responsibility *in loco parentis* by protecting its students from subversive ideas. The university president and his minions were evidently surprised by the intensity of protest against the rule, and they responded with the strategy of shock and awe introduced by President Truman at Hiroshima. At that time Ohio's 88 county agricultural agents were members of the university faculty, along with a cohort of Columbus MD's who were adjunct professors of medicine. So the president called a meeting of the entire faculty, its first for a century, at which attendance was mandated for every agricultural agent and adjunct professor of medicine. The idea was to intimidate the protesters by demonstrating for all to see how few and marginal we really were. But to the administration's shock and awe when the vote was taken, 509 people, one third of those present, stood up to be counted in open defiance of our president. (Eight years later this martinet, Novice G. Fawcett, was to preside over the National Guard's occupation of the campus following a student "riot" he had every reason to know was initiated by plainclothes Columbus police.)

During the two years following the speakers' rule meeting, the Ohio State English department experienced a mass exodus of faculty. California and New York were then expanding their university systems with multiple new campuses, and when our Roy Harvey Pearce was invited to create from scratch the Department of Literature at LaJolla, he chose for its nucleus three Ohio State colleagues. Others soon went to Irvine, Riverside (Don Howard), San Francisco State, and the new SUNY campuses, and several of the departees made the speakers' episode their avowed reason for leaving. One of them, my friend Eric Solomon, published an account of the controversy in *The Atlantic Monthly*, and it took Ohio State years to recover from this public relations disaster.

But another reason for these departures was bi-coastal geography and money, and it did not occur to the departing to ask us they were leaving behind whether we wanted the help they thought they were giving us. They in fact made it harder on us, and the irony was that as soon as our Californians got settled in their new jobs, Ronald Reagan was elected their governor, and the ensuing Berkeley free-speech controversy that consumed California was just a flamboyant reprise of what they'd said they were fleeing at Ohio State.

This faculty exodus marked Ohio State's transition from an Old Left preoccupied by its resistance to McCarthyism to a New Left in full rebellion at the national Establishment. When the now discredited Novice Fawcett announced his retirement a year after the strike, one of my new young colleagues, Tom Mitchell, persuaded me to be spokesperson for a student delegation that he and I led to a meeting of the university's Board of Trustees where anyone wishing to nominate a new president would be permitted to do so. I was required to apply two weeks in advance for a place on the meeting agenda, and I was notified I'd be allotted 5 minutes by a note slipped under my office door at 7 a.m. on the morning of the meeting.

When I arrived at this meeting in my best suit and necktie with Tom in his blue jeans and a score of shaggy students, he and the students were told to wait in the corridor outside the meeting room, where they promptly sat on the floor. I was ushered into this room where the trustees were seated at a U-shaped table under the blazing lights of TV cameras, and we humble petitioners were seated across in rows of outer darkness. When I was called on to come forward with my heart pounding and knees shaking, I looked pointedly at Novice Fawcett and then turned to argue that it was time for Ohio State to have innovative leadership instead of bureaucratic management. With suitable encomiums I nominated the attorney Staughton Lynd, a national hero of the labor, civil rights, and anti-war movements, for president of our university. This was loudly applauded by the students in the hallway, and I was unforgettably thanked by the chairman of the Board of Trustees: "At a great university like Ohio State," he said, "we recognize that everyone has the right to an opinion, and we are grateful to hear yours, Professor." Whereupon I receded into the darkness.

We didn't get Staughton Lynd, but we did get Harold Enarson, who, as president at Cleveland State during its 1970 uprising, had been far more responsive, transparent, and effective in resolving his crisis than Novice Fawcett propped up at his impasse by the Ohio National Guard. Then for the next decade, 1972-81, Enarson presided over a deep transformation of university government and culture with the indispensable help of our Al Kuhn as his provost. Students and faculty gained new voice, and the university's scholarly range and curriculum were greatly broadened. Most notably for people like me, Ohio State's Black

Studies and Women's Studies programs were established, with their grounding in what was soon called "identity politics," and in response to that I felt deeply divided.

On the one hand, my inner marxist was ecstatic over the scholarly agenda and curricular reform which the new programs staked out. Now at last, what the Communist Party had called "the Negro Question" and "the Woman Question" were becoming mainstream questions for the academy as well as the nation. On the other hand, my inner marxist was distraught by the new scholarship's evasion of class as a question inseparable from those of race and gender. What the new movement really aimed at is what Paul Goodman, one of its original gurus and eventual critics, called in the title of his 1970 book a *"New Reformation."* "By 'Reformation'," Goodman explained, "I mean simply an upheaval of belief that is of religious depth, but that does *not* involve destroying the common faith, but to purge and reform it" [sic]. The common faith he referred to was America's faith in "scientific technology," but his remark applied also to our faith in capitalism, which the movement often mocked but which it never engaged in the way it engaged racism, sexism, and militarism. And despite a lot of lip service over the next forty years, this evasion has continued while identities have multiplied. The academy now boasts specialists by thousands in Asian studies, GLT studies, Latino/a studies, Native American studies, and multicultural studies, but barely a handful in proletarian studies. It still hasn't found a way to become serious about class.

Then there was a third hand, on which my inner aesthetician felt threatened by the movement's attack on the artistic standards by which I'd been leading first-generation college students to understand Shakespeare, Melville, and Dostoevsky in something approaching their full depth and power. These were now uniformly condemned as elite white male standards, and they seemed often to include the analytical coherence and clarity of expression (aka "linear thinking") that I'd been trying to cultivate in my students' writing. For all that I shared of the New Left's anti-Establishment critique, my two poles of intellectual attraction, to class expropriation and artistic form, were both repellent to its leading scholars and ideologues.

Two experiences during these years, both involving the civil rights movement, led me to accept identity politics as inevitable despite my deep misgivings. During the late 60s, Gordon, Joan, and I had participated in various off-campus civil rights activities, Gordon and I going to mass demonstrations in New York and Washington while Joan and I joined the local chapter of CORE (Committee on Racial Equality), which had maybe a dozen members who picketed apartment buildings that refused black tenants. I also taught a class in English grammar and usage to black adults trying to pass the high school equivalency exam so as to qualify for jobs as supermarket cashiers. Here I thought was something urgent in which I could also sustain at home the feeling of solidarity I'd experienced with 100,000 people at those east coast demonstrations. During the "Mississippi Summer" of 1964 my brother Chuck spent a month in Jackson providing legal protection to civil rights activists, and then back in Chicago initiated a historic lawsuit against the Chicago Housing Authority for warehousing black people in high-rise housing projects. My sister Mimi was a notorious Chicago activist, and the least I could do was make an effort in Columbus.

But it turned out that teaching black people the Standard English of the high school equivalency exam was hugely frustrating. I'd been effortlessly successful in doing this with the National Secretaries Association just a few years earlier, and now it was like pulling teeth. In near desperation, I followed a hunch that perhaps memory flatters me as working better than it did. I distributed in class John Donne's Holy Sonnet "Death be not proud," and I performed a detailed analysis of this poem in the manner of the New Critics. The students' "Eureka!" response to my analysis revealed the underlying language comprehension I had so far failed to impart, and the weekly lessons became more productive after that. Most of them passed the equivalency exam, and I'll never be sure what happened. Maybe it was that a poem about death led them to trust me for the first time and begin paying attention, or maybe it went something like this: the language of Donne's poem is far from Standard English, but his Christian struggle to come to terms with death was powerfully moving to these deeply devout people, and when they saw how his poem's deviations produced its emotional effect, they also had to see, linguistically speaking, where those deviations were coming from.

This experience showed me starkly how culturally far apart most whites and blacks really were, and it prompted me to question the ethics of imposing on blacks a cultural exam that was stacked against them for no functional reason that I could identify. Like John Donne, they had an expressive language of their own, which since that time has permeated Standard English, so what did they need me for? To help put them in their place as supermarket cashiers? They were asking themselves these same questions, and the sequel to my teaching the equivalency exam was my being kicked out of the civil rights movement, along with all the other whites, upon the advent of Black Power.

At a packed meeting attended by maybe three times as many people as our original CORE membership, there was a sharp debate in which one after another black speaker explained, some fiercely and some with icy calm, how in present circumstances our white good will couldn't help but be racist, and how they had to find their identity and future through their own will and process. As Barack Obama was later to explain it in *Dreams From My Father*, "if he [the white man] treated you like a man or came to your defense, it was because he knew that the words you spoke, the clothes you wore, the books you read, your ambitions and desires, were already his. Whatever he decided to do, it was his decision to make, not yours..." That description fits me in my eagerness to impart Standard English, and, shaken as I was when they asked us whites to leave the meeting then and there, I had to accept their insistence on identity politics. But of course that wasn't the end of it, and in the following years I was to clash more than once with the university's Black Establishment over its resolute separatism in pursuing a phantasm of identity

7.

On our climbing trip that included the Mount Wilson traverse, Joan and I were camped above tree line for a week, and I let my beard grow rather than shave in cold water. When we got down I decided to keep it growing, and from that time until I went totally bald, people kept telling me I looked just like the poet Alan Ginsburg, a compliment I remained unable to appreciate. When Gordon Grigsby came to Boulder the summer we hatched our teaching experiment, he and I took a three-day backpacking trip, where, from supper until dark each evening, we two flaming leftists played mumbly-peg, a boy's game of territorial conquest achieved by throwing strategically aimed pocket knives into the contested ground, which he'd grown up with in Philadelphia and I in Chicago. And over the 1973 Thanksgiving weekend, we two drove to New York State to explore the possibility of buying an abandoned Catskill resort in which to start a college. Although promising change was now in process at Ohio State, we still dreamed of creating a face-to-face community free of bureaucratic infrastructure. We had lined up appointments with local real estate agents, and we had piqued the interest of colleagues in the sciences who might be willing to join us in offering an unemcumbered liberal education.

We stopped overnight in Ithaca, where a former student of Gordon's was now a graduate student at Cornell, and she took us to a faculty-student party whose rarefied air left me relieved that I'd declined an invitation to negotiate a job with Cornell when Joan and I were courting. Next afternoon, at a nicely preserved Catskill resort that looked feasible for our purpose and perhaps affordable if our science colleagues joined in, we got around to asking the real estate agent what was the average annual snowfall. When he said 120 inches, we pondered becoming skiers for maybe three minutes, and then gave up on the whole fantasy.

Back in Columbus, Gordon and I pioneered team-teaching in the English department, for which there was then no budget. My salary being higher than his, we got the team-taught course entered on my schedule, and I paid him half my salary for that course. I was then also paying child support for Rachel, and for the three months I wrote Gordon checks, I cooked a lot of socialistic brown rice. But our venture helped leverage the university into financing team teaching, whose educational value it came to recognize for a few years. Tom Mitchell and Marlene Longenecker followed us at full salary for both, then others as well, and by the time I retired I had also team-taught with three other people. But team-teaching now has gone by the boards with the university's adoption of an "enrollment-driven" budget model.

In the pain of my separation from Joan, I lost a lot of sleep, took a lot of valium, and did a lot of lonely walking. During this time my brother Chuck committed suicide, leaving a wife and three sons, and I sometimes had that thought. I had a couple of brief encounters with other women, and then two people came into the forefront of my life never to leave, Jim Kincaid and Robin Bell. Jim was one of Al Kuhn's first hires, but he and I only became friends following the teaching experiment, where he'd been excited by what Gordon, Joan, and I were attempting at just the moment when, himself newly tenured, he could let his inner iconoclast out of the closet. At the department meeting where our teaching experiment was debated, one of our traditionalist critics, the endearing and soft-spoken Ed Robbins, made a perfectly predictable argument against letting the students choose what to read and write and then assign their own grades. He was answered by Jim, whose first words were "Nobody thinks that way anymore, do they?", and neither Ed Robbins nor anyone else was the least bit put off by these words. We all knew they were not personal but rhetorical, and from there Jim has gone on rattling ideological cages, most gratefully mine, on his way to becoming one of America's rare public intellectuals to emerge from the wisdom of the humanities.

He and I went on to team-teach a seminar in Dickens and Melville where we argued our divergent views over a rambunctious ten weeks that became legendary among graduate students. We followed this with thirty years of debating in long letters the theory of literature and the state of our profession, sharpening each other's thinking while also saving each other from our worst excesses. (Well, he at least saved me.) Here is one of many glories of the life of the mind that the American university makes possible: we were not Einstein and Bohr at one of their legendary Solvay conferences but just two academic proles being afforded every day the space to be self-critical about what we were doing.

Jim is a rabid sports fan, just like Robin, and they both grew up in the environs of Pittsburgh as fanatics of the Pirates in baseball and the Steelers in football. I'd once had an attachment like theirs to Chicago's Cubs and Bears, but upon getting a Ph.D. I'd put away such childish things. They never did, and now they revived me just in time for the Steelers' great run of four NFL championships from 1974 to 1979. On Sundays when the Steelers were on local TV, we three would gather in my apartment with a six-pack and burn more adrenalin than we'd done all week long in the classroom. We yelled, stomped, groaned, and gut-wrenched those Steel Curtain teams to victory, and by Sunday evening we were totally drained for Monday's classes.

I'd met Robin on the volleyball court, and this led to our stopping to talk when we ran into each other on campus. She was a graduate student who had never taken a class with me (many took two) because, as I was later to learn, she wasn't really interested in the stuff I taught. Her conversation was even so sharp and provocative, and one thing led to another as we discovered ourselves to be opposites that attract. Where I spend my waking hours among the cloudy abstractions of political theory and literary form, she spends hers among the quotidian practices of gardening, cooking, woodcarving, and bird watching. Where I search for life's meaning in master narratives by Marx, Spengler, or Jared Diamond, she gives life meaning one day at a time, and her scholarship is just one aspect of this. Her M.A. thesis on Virginia Woolf quietly anticipated Woolf's re-discovery by second-wave feminism, and by the time her Ph.D. dissertation became a prize-winning book on paragraph cohesion, she'd forgotten all about it amidst the pressing concerns of transplanting hostas and sighting magnolia warblers.

I was now very frightened of failing in marriage a third time, and where that is concerned I dragged my feet in more hurtful ways than I want to remember. But I finally asked Joan for a divorce, and we bought a 100-year-old house for which we had to borrow even the down payment from friends. We began with just the clothes on our backs and the barebones furniture of our two apartments, and for the first couple of pay periods we counted change before going to the supermarket. We also had our biggest fight then or since, over whether to get a dog to go with Robin's cat. I prevailed, no dog, and once past that, the bumps that followed led us to grow more together. On weekends her parents came over from Pittsburgh to help us get settled, and we soon realized they were finding ways not to stay overnight until after the wedding. That occurred in December, 1978, two years into my first term as chair of the English department.

It had taken me these twenty years, between arriving at Ohio State in 1956 and becoming department chair in 1976, to find my center of gravity both personally and professionally. I had worked through a heap of emotional trauma while also bringing into focus my intellectual excitement, and by now I had some inner authority. The pain of my personal life, in which I had to see how much hurt I inflicted while also being hurt, had partly healed and partly calloused, to a point where you could perhaps say I had become a little more mature. And in my professional life I had become a presence in teaching and service while also laying the groundwork for scholarship in which I might also become the thinker I aspired to be. Any growth from now on could be an organic unfolding from within rather than a sporadic groping from without, and while I still had much to learn, I was now embarking on that with some buoyancy.

CHAPTER 5. ADVENTURE IN MIDDLE MANAGEMENT:

COLUMBUS, 1976-83

When I became chair of the Ohio State English department on July 1, 1976, a week after my 51st birthday, I'd been a member of the department for twenty years. I'd been its Executive Secretary, Vice-Chair, and at one time or another chair of its internal governance and policy committees. I'd been on high-level college and university committees, and between my classroom experience and my psychotherapy experience, I had learned the value of listening and the value of transparency. But my record of political activism in both the department and university had also marked me as a radical, and this led to some initial complications. Most of our new generation were of the 60s New Left, while many of our older generation had been upset by my overheated response to the 1970 strike. Insofar as I was both old and left, I suppose I was seen by some as a bridge between generations. But even where I was personally liked, I'm sure that many thought it still too soon, if ever, for me to overcome my reputation as a rabble rouser.

Not only were there two other candidates, but my sponsor Jim Kincaid insisted I make a campaign stop at the department's long-standing monthly poker game, in which I had never participated. I am a profoundly inept poker player, but that night the cards kept falling my way, and I came home with $40 in spite of myself, a big pot by the standards of that game. It was the most embarrassing evening of my life. But I scored points for my good will, and I was forgiven my luck when the departmental search committee ended up ranking me first among the candidates.

A department chair is officially appointed by the college dean, and our dean had asked this committee for an unranked list of three names from which to make his choice, a not unusual practice in that era. But in this case it seemed clear that the dean's request was aimed at enabling him to bypass me with my swarthy beard and claque of tie-dyed supporters. This dean, Arthur Adams, was a fellow WWII veteran whose military career and bearing couldn't be more different from mine. He was a broad-shouldered, skin-headed Soviet historian who'd been a member of the Special Service Forces (aka spy) and was even now, according to rumor, a Cold War consultant to the CIA. So our search committee decided to send him one name only, mine as the department's first choice, take it or leave it. When he then called the committee chair to his office and asked for two more names, Bob Jones stood firm, and Adams apparently decided not to force this soon again the sort of confrontation he'd just had with our Black Studies Department.

He promptly sat me down in his dim-lit, dark-curtained office for a laying-on of hands, and he began with two admonitions. First he said, "I know all you people in English are passionate about departmental democracy, but over here in the College it's all feudalism. You swear loyalty to me, and I swear to support you." Then he said, "I know all you people in English really love words, but over here in the College we always have too much to read, and I don't want ever to receive from you any letter—hiring request, budget request, tenure or promotion recommendation—more than two pages long." I swore my oaths, he swore his, and we soon developed a strong working rapport during what turned out to be his last year as dean. Adams was one of those no-minced-words WASPS whom I'd always found intimidating but who was now to my surprise an open-minded listener. Once he reassured himself that I was actually interested in learning the job and not just in disrupting the system, he gave me his confidence, along with a lot of "tough love" criticism. He and his staff made me a quick learner, and he began by adding two big items to the department's agenda for my first year—a self-study of our entire operation, top to bottom, culminating in site visits by outside evaluators; and the establishment of a new program in remedial writing (as it was then called), which had just been recommended in a committee report he had commissioned.

Departmental self-study was then becoming a nationwide practice, and it could be perceived as just one more hoop wrought by administrators for faculty to jump through in order to justify the administrators' existence. But I embraced it (as did most of my colleagues) as an opportunity to look at ourselves in a collective spirit of self-criticism at the beginning of my tenure as chair. For one thing, it could be used to hasten the process, already under way, of incorporating in our teaching, research, and service some of the ideas and spirit of the 60s—a broadened and more flexible curriculum, a more interactive pedagogy, a more widely representative departmental government. That would be an auspicious beginning for me, and, since we were to be the first department in the university to do a self-study, I thought the money pot would be full enough to implement any recommendations we might produce. Which it was.

The remedial writing project, on the other hand, gave me the jitters. It implied a curriculum and pedagogy rigidly defined rather than flexible and free-wheeling, and I was the one who'd proclaimed at our 1970 meeting that I didn't care if my students submitted paintings or songs to satisfy their writing requirement. Not only would I now have to eat those words but also, in so doing, bring to the surface the underlying rift between literature and composition that constantly plagues English departments in public universities. I anticipated that negotiating this rift would set a tone for my tenure as chair, and it did. When I came up for re-election four years later, the dean at that time conferred with my colleagues before reappointing me, and he told me that their one big criticism of my first-term performance was that I spent too much time on our writing program. Or as the old joke goes, an English department chair dies, goes to heaven, and is greeted by St. Peter at the Pearly Gates. "You've lived an honorable life," says Peter, "and you are eligible to enter. But I should also mention that if you should choose to enter rather than be hurled down below, you will still be held responsible for the writing program."

Yet I also sensed that this program could be an opportunity as well as a burden. Neither by temperament nor ambition was I the person to lead my department in a scholarly charge to the cutting edge of literary theory. My ambition was to make a difference in the daily life where our professional work was grounded, and the study and teaching of writing had always been a big part of this life. Indeed, in the American university's postwar prosperity, the first relief sought by English professors was relief from teaching so much writing. Ten years after I was grading 104 themes every ten days, no new faculty taught a freshman English class, and many universities had outsourced the teaching of writing to an exploited cadre of finely qualified teachers drawn from the reserve army of the unemployed. My predecessors in the chair had worked to keep folklore and creative writing within the English department, not just administratively but also intellectually, and this had enriched our collective life by keeping us, as Malory wrote of the Round Table at Camelot, "all whole together." The study and teaching of writing felt this way to me, and engaging the difficulties involved in keeping it at the table did not seem beneath the dignity of an aspiring socialist. It just turned out to take an awful lot of doing.

Here perhaps is why so many left academics condescend to administrators as glorified secretaries and bean counters. We on the left are long-practiced at what Robert Hughes called "the culture of complaint"; we are never without a list of grievances (most of them justified) at the inequities endemic to capitalism, and we organize and petition for redress of these grievances. But we decline by and large to dirty our hands by pursuing our own goals in the messy, wasteful, bureaucratic infighting through which capitalism can still accommodate our principles in some very substantial ways. I knew, for example, that a lot of my energy would have to be focused on infrastructure maintenance that is indifferently political. But a leftist is not only more alert than a bureaucrat to protect the teaching of writing from becoming alienated labor; she is also more likely to support a secretary negotiating a transcontinental divorce initiated by the husband she'd put through medical school and borne two children. Even an equipment budget can be political: when I managed to get annual allotments to put electric typewriters in faculty offices, I began with the lowest-ranking faculty.

A larger opportunity the chair's position offers an aspiring socialist is the academy's long tradition of departmental self-management. The academic workplace is exceptional within capitalism insofar as university faculties consist mostly of people paid to do something they love doing and, in trying to do it well, hold themselves accountable to each other through peer evaluation and self-government. Their ethics look toward what we socialists idealize for society as a whole, and if there were ever an opportunity to test this ideal, the chair's job was it.

This job stands at the intersection between a face-to-face departmental community capable of self-management, and a distant hierarchy of deans, provosts, presidents, and trustees acculturated in what Art Adams called the politics of feudalism. After that first talk with Adams, I'd come back to my big new office, one side of which was a bank of windows looking out onto green space, and literally trembled for the best part of an hour. I felt on familiar ground in trying to deepen participatory democracy in the everyday life of my department. But I had no clear idea of how, or how far, I could protect the communal processes of the department from the authoritarian processes of our institutional lords. In the 1970 strike, I had observed a paralyzing syndrome in the university's best-hearted middle managers, which I came to call the crucifixion reflex. These people felt caught between a sympathetic recognition that the students' calls for change were justified and a frightened recognition that, no matter how compelling the students' arguments might be, the university administration would not tolerate a challenge to its authority coming from below. Their way up to this cross was to tell the students their goals were laudable but they were using the wrong tactics to achieve them. Leave it to us in our agony, they said, to negotiate your concerns through the established channels of communication and decision-making. But even when they succeeded in doing this, which wasn't often, it took months (or years) of haggling in which nothing essential was said that hadn't been anticipated by the original petitioners. Functionally speaking, the process of moving up the hierarchy did not produce a cooler or deeper consideration of the problem at hand. It compounded the problem by denying the petitioners any experience of democratic accomplishment while also reassuring the top dogs that their power was intact.

As I stared out the window during that first trembling hour, I knew I didn't want to be subject to this crucifixion reflex. Nor did I want to become a merely symbolic witness to my principles without taking the risk of trying to implement them. I remembered how Bob Estrich, the chairman I idolized and most wanted to emulate, made his great 1962 speech to the faculty in protest of the "speakers' rule" only after the vote had been taken to enforce the rule. Some at that meeting were inspired for life by Estrich's Jeffersonian eloquence on behalf of free speech. But it could have cost him all further effectiveness in his job to have spoken before the vote was taken, while his words still had some chance of influencing the outcome. I didn't want to find myself in that position either, and I sat there wondering which of my principles I'd be willing to compromise, and by how much, before recognizing it was time to offer my resignation. Finally I remembered some middle managers who pursued grass roots issues as a matter of everyday leadership, and this helped me to stop my melodramatic trembling. And as things turned out, on at least three occasions during my seven years I got myself ready to resign if necessary.

2.

It took me two years to master the annual administrative cycle: tenure in the autumn, hiring and budget in the winter, promotion in the spring, scheduling in the summer. Along with that came the daily carnival of inviting opportunities, hair's breadth escapes, modest victories, and total defeats. My eloquence failed to persuade my colleagues to accept the dean's proposal that we bring into the English department the struggling interdisciplinary Division of Comparative Studies. I now proclaimed by executive fiat that everyone must teach one writing course a year and also require x amount of writing in their literature classes. An all-American football player threatened his female freshman English teacher, and I stormed into their classroom the next day and in sheer bravado asked him before all present if he wanted to deal with me or the police. We initiated a department colloquium in which to present to each other our work in progress. An African-American professor fraudulently played the affirmative-action card while accusing me of racism. Jim Kincaid accepted a job at Colorado, and for a fatuous half-hour I let myself believe I had persuaded Tom Mitchell to remain at Ohio State rather than go to Chicago and become editor of *Critical Inquiry*. A faculty wife surgeon gave the department its first Xerox machine in honor of her husband's birthday, and this socialist restricted its use to faculty but not graduate students or we couldn't afford the paper.

And a beloved colleague whose marriage broke up began coming to class drunk at 10 a.m. and soon committed suicide.

An assistant attorney general called to ask whether a comma in one sentence might leave the state of Ohio liable for $1,000,000. A university trustee chided me that our first-ever course in gay literature would drive students away, to which I replied that on the contrary it would attract them, and it did. I instituted a program of exchange teaching with faculty at our satellite two-year campuses. I failed to persuade my colleagues to hire two women who later became distinguished scholars. I wrote a famous memo on sexual harassment, scolding the men for telling sexist jokes in the elevators and also the women for finding offense under every stone. An irate father called to protest his daughter's exposure to obscenity in her folklore class, and I gave him a reasoned earful about academic freedom and the integrity of scholarship. A memo from the provost warned that tenured positions might be eliminated in response to the latest state budget, but the next budget was bountiful, and I got money for typewriters in faculty offices. And in my vanity as a graduate of the Pellin Institute, on a gorgeous spring afternoon I undertook a two-hour therapy session with a highly talented, deeply neurotic undergraduate sitting on the front steps of his dilapidated rooming house. Just when I thought I had saved him for college life and English Literature, he grabbed my arm and bit me.

My first response to the daily excitement and stress was neurotic eating. My second was to take up cigar smoking to offset the eating, and my third was to resume aerobic swimming to flush out the nicotine and tar. My cigar of choice was El Producto, of which I became a chain-smoker at 65c for a packet of five. I'd light the first one after breakfast at home and the second on reaching the office at 7.30 a.m. My first sign that Art Adams approved of my performance was when he took me to lunch and afterwards bought me an 85c cigar, and my last act as chair was to wash my office windows encrusted with seven years' exhalation. I quit cigars the next day, and it took Robin six weeks to notice.

Fidel Castro advised Hugo Chavez that in pursuing his Bolivarian Revolution, he could not allow himself to become "mayor of Venezuela," and in a department now the size of a small college, I didn't need any prompting to depend on the decentralized committee process by which we had come long ago to delegate democratic authority. But I also needed to depend on some people day by day, and the two who helped me most to get through those first two years were John Muste and Pattie Dodd. John had come to Ohio State two years after I did, and we were now longtime friends. He was a founder of the poker game and also department vice-chair, and I had asked him to stay on and help me learn the ropes. He was a towering man, maybe 6'6", who'd played basketball as an undergraduate at Brown, contracted polio on his honeymoon, and got his Ph.D. at Wisconsin. He used arm canes that came to my shoulders, and in applying for a disability parking permit he was required every year to climb stairs to the second floor of our administration building and give ocular proof of his disability to the former FBI agent in charge of such matters.

John endured this and other indignities with amazing grace. I never saw in him a trace of frustration with his paralysis, or of bitterness at just missing the advent of the Salk vaccine. His father was the world famous pacifist and socialist, and while John didn't share A.J.'s politics, he'd inherited his spirit. He'd been a wise and caring adviser when I turned to him in the pain of my separation from Joan, and now I kept trying out on John the strategies I was contemplating for use on the job. Not only did he shepherd me through the established routines, but he analyzed precisely the risks involved in following some of my wilder impulses. He saved me from myself more often than I want to remember, and my first hard decision was to ask him to leave the vice-chair's position and return to the faculty during my second year. Not only were we deeply comfortable working together, but it was becoming harder for him each year to stand before his classes as a full-time teacher. Yet I thought it was time to break the department's tradition of white male administrators, and John couldn't help but agree. Happily for all concerned, he was soon appointed associate dean of the College, a job in which he thrived until retiring, and meanwhile I asked Marlene Longenecker to become vice-chair.

Pattie Dodd, our newest secretary barely out of high school, was also the only one who knew shorthand. I'd thought about getting a tape recorder, but I am even more inept with electronic devices than I am at poker, so I started practicing dictation with

Pattie. I'm an obsessive reviser, and in no time she was giving me typed drafts I could tinker with. But well beyond that, Pattie was the first of many people I was now to encounter who exfoliate and blossom as soon as you give them the chance. She was smart, observant, and totally lacking in self-confidence, like so many of our land-grant students. When I told her my letters could be two pages max, she suggested some ways to make my prose more straightforward and Anglo-Saxon. When I had her attend department meetings to take minutes (an unprecedented breach of the inner sanctum by the lower orders), she was a step ahead of my signal in recognizing what she needed to record. She made shrewd judgments of people and offered telling suggestions for negotiating the interpersonal bumps. And when her short-lived marriage broke up during my second year, she came into my office sobbing to tell me that her husband had left her and thereby proved that she was as unattractive and boring as she had always known. I tried to persuade her otherwise (I found her so attractive I'd thought twice about asking her to work with me), but I also knew well how trauma like this can't be healed just by words. It takes time, and two years later I was recommending Pattie for a job as secretary to an Indiana Supreme Court justice. She moved to Indianapolis, we lost touch, and here was the first of many wrenches I was to have in losing a workmate-become-friend because she took the opportunity she was given to grow into herself.

3.

Someone suggested that we launch our self-study with a weekend retreat at a state park before the new school year began. There was no budget for this, nor was there any precedent at that time for an off campus retreat. But to my surprise, people agreed to pay their own way, and we devoted each half-day's session at the retreat to a single aspect of the department's work: teaching; scholarship; undergraduate, graduate, and writing programs; departmental organization and government. The idea was to agree for each area on a general critique and guidelines for reform, on which Pattie took copious notes, and then to develop detailed proposals within these guidelines after we got home.

In ways I could never have anticipated, this retreat was a landmark event in the history of the department, far more valuable than the self-study report it produced, and it set the tone for my seven years as chair. Not only were our discussions productive, but outside the meeting room people who'd been at best polite acquaintances engaged each other's humanity for perhaps the first time. Old timers and newcomers, scotch-drinkers and pot smokers, medievalists and Americanists, grilled food together and shared cabins in the woods and canoes on the lake. Some uptight liberals were persuaded to smoke a joint, and some shaggy insurgents were persuaded by the arguments of rock-ribbed conservatives. We had fun while engaging serious issues, on which people worked to find compromises that didn't threaten their principles. Thirty years later people still reminisce about that retreat.

A deepened community spirit carried over when we got back, which I tried to sustain first of all by my conduct of routine department business. Prominent here was my use of Roberts Rules of Order, in imitation of the AVC's Morris Pottish thirty years ago, to make our deliberations at meetings more thorough, focused, and efficient. These rules provide for a systematic presentation of the arguments on any issue before a formal vote is taken, which makes it more likely that when the vote is taken it will reflect an informed consensus. I stumbled with this at first, but my colleagues recognized my good will and gave me their patience, until over time we developed a collective discipline that led academics, of all people, to say they liked coming to meetings.

It's a great irony that so many people who espouse participatory democracy, whether academics or socialists or multitudinarians, are so inept at participation when the time actually comes. Rosa Luxemburg, perhaps the greatest marxist after Marx, wrote to a friend from prison that she got more inner satisfaction from the prison garden than "from one of our party congresses." Participatory discussion becomes too often a speechifying free-for-all where everyone gets to say her piece, but only in incoherent sequences that maximize repetition, confusion, frustration, and drowsiness. The first thing I learned was to separate the overlapping issues involved in any discussion and then rule people out of order as soon as they strayed from the issue at hand. The second was to cut people off as soon as it became clear they were repeating what others had already said. The third was to voice my own position as forcefully as I could while also conducting the meeting with exaggerated impartiality and remaining genuinely cheerful (most of the time) when my position was outvoted, which happened quite often.

Then there was the tactic I grew into by stages, which walks a fine line between cultivating democratic participation and stacking the meeting. David Frantz, my vice chair by that time, called it "lining up your ducks." In a face-to-face community, people's opinions on most issues become over time largely predictable. We all know who belongs to the left, right, and center, who has hot buttons, who is outspoken and who reticent, whose head is always in the sand, and whose stentorian voice always seems to carry more weight. I began studying the department roster and anticipating where individuals would stand on some issue in which I was invested—a curriculum revision, degree requirement, promotion or salary recommendation. Then I would stop privately by the office of one I thought was wavering on this issue and try to persuade her, or one who I thought agreed with me already but would be reluctant to speak up. "You know how vociferous X is going to be on this at the meeting, but what X doesn't realize is the crucial importance of blah blah blah." I got my way often, and when I didn't I demonstrated that there would be no retribution.

While a tactic like this can be devious, it can also help cultivate an active practice of participation, and with me it was some of both. Then at the meeting, when discussion on the issue ended, the voting followed Roberts Rules for initial motions, amendments, substitute motions, and motions to table. These facilitate a fully considered outcome, and after a few repetitions we began to thrive on the process. People came away more often than not feeling satisfied for having heard the relevant arguments as (more or less) coherent wholes, and for having arrived at a definitive result for this particular group at this particular time. I came away feeling that participatory democracy must become above all an internalized and reinforced discipline, like passing the basketball, which we are all capable of learning.

My efforts to make it so were augmented by others. Stanley Kahrl, a Harvard-bred traditionalist with a book-bag, made several new proposals, all adopted, for conducting our meetings on the life-and-death question of tenure and promotion. The most valuable of these for me was that decision-making on tenure and promotion be broken into four stages—an informal discussion culminating in a preliminary straw vote by secret ballot to see where we stood; then a formal motion; then further discussion only if there was something still to be said that really had a chance of changing people's minds; and then a final vote by an open show of hands. God is in the details, and Stanley gave us a way both not to waste words and not to hide from each other. He argued that we must face each other openly as members of a community united in long-range purpose, and for me this echoed the United Front ideal of people working toward a common goal in the clear light of their avowed differences.

4.

The department self-study, carried out over the 1976-7 and 1977-8 academic years, produced a preliminary 67-page report sent to our three outside examiners in advance of their campus visit, which turned out to be the weekend of Columbus's great blizzard of '78, twenty-seven inches of snow in three days. The classes we had arranged for them to attend were cancelled, but not the dinner parties at faculty homes, and what I remember most about the self-study is spending our evenings that weekend pushing cars out of snow banks. But we did produce a "Memorandum of Agreement" with the College for implementing a list of mundane recommendations—to finance training sessions for new TA's; to institute university-wide faculty seminars on assigning and grading writing; to undertake interdisciplinary courses with other departments; to continue the process, well under way before I became chair, of incorporating in our curriculum the new directions in our discipline heralded by the 60s —black studies, women's studies, genre studies; literary, rhetorical, and cultural theory. Our department had been until then a bit hidebound in scholarly range: our strengths were in literary history, medieval literature, and textual editing. But the self-study report notes that "Among eight new colleagues hired during the last two years, five are primarily theoreticians, rhetoricians, genre critics, or interdisciplinary scholars, and we now have appropriate courses for them to teach." And among the six people we hired in my first year, two were literary theorists, one an interdisciplinary scholar, one a medievalist, one a modernist, and one the director of our new remedial writing program. We were catching up with new developments in literary and rhetorical theory while also making our writing curriculum one of the most comprehensive and well articulated in the country.

The self-study, like the retreat that initiated it, was a deeply communal experience and accomplishment. Although its recommendations were anything but ground-breaking, they brought a surge of morale in our manner of reaching them, and that got my chairmanship off on the terrain that I cared most about.

5.

During my years as chair Ohio State was still accepting for admission anyone with a high school diploma. This included large numbers of students who could neither write basic English nor perform basic algebra, and our mathematics department was instituting a remedial program in tandem with ours. I secured a budget that allowed us to hire full-time staff on three-year renewable appointments at livable salaries that included benefits, along with a few tenure-track positions for scholars of rhetoric and composition. These were at first controversial partly because they involved diversions of job slots, and also because we had no settled criteria for the hiring and promotion of people in rhetoric and composition.

Literary scholars have a long tradition, from which I at that time was certainly not exempt, of intellectual condescension toward rhetoric and composition. Make-work scholarship occurs in all fields, but here it had always seemed to me disproportionate. Yet Robin was just then writing her Ph.D. dissertation on cohesion in the English paragraph, and there was no way I could condescend to the linguistic and rhetorical knowledge, or the methodological sophistication, that I saw both in her manuscript drafts and in select work by others in her field.

I also knew politically that if I didn't want my chairmanship to end before it began, we couldn't afford to follow the suggestion of some that we defy the dean and his three-R's mentality by refusing to establish remedial writing. I argued that in taking on this pedagogical challenge we could also give ourselves the scholarly challenge of cultivating a research field closely connected with our land-grant mission, and this argument helped secure the budget that provided our new writing staff a measure of job security. If composition pedagogy was now to be dignified as a research field with tenure-track job slots, then the classroom teaching of writing could no more be left than the teaching of Milton to what our administration called "casuals" (i.e., part-timers).

Looking back now, I think all I did was put a finger in the dike. Those renewable appointments were certainly not equivalent to tenure-track positions, and they have meanwhile become an anomaly. In today's corporatized university, where the rewards for scholarship as compared with teaching are more disproportionate than ever, the teaching of writing still counts least of all. One irony in this has always been that low-paid writing instruction helps support high-paid research production. But there is now perhaps a further irony, that the establishment of composition pedagogy and "literacy studies" as research specialties has coincided with the casualization of instruction in writing—as if research publication on writing has become a fig leaf for consigning the teaching of writing to exploited part-timers.

Our new remedial "Writing Workshop" was quickly successful in qualifying students to go on to freshman English, just like our established ESL program. Then over several years we added a drop-in "Writing Skills Lab," which offered grammatical and rhetorical first aid to every scrivener in the university (including faculty), along with an array of advanced courses in research & term paper writing, technical writing, and business & professional writing to go with our existing courses in critical and expository writing. Working to establish this comprehensive program was what my colleagues had in mind when they said I spent too much time on rhetoric and composition. For it was not just that our literature faculty had to be persuaded to support equal eminence for scholars of rhetoric and composition, but also that the rhetoricians had to be constantly rescued from their ineptitude at persuasion. At the day-long retreat where we adopted the new writing courses, these people kept putting their feet in their mouths, and I was at my wit's end pleading their case on their behalf.

Delegating administration of our writing program also proved a formidable task. Back then, the reputations of rhetoric and composition scholars outran not only their sense of audience but also their capacity to pay attention to detail. I shudder to remember that during one period I had David Frantz sit in on my meetings with our Director of Writing, whose dropped balls I was regularly picking up, so as to keep me from yelling at him one more time. But I also glow to remember with affection two administrative subordinates in our writing program, Ron Fortune and Susan Helgeson, whose professional knowledge, effortless diplomacy, and hands-on attention went far to offset their bosses' bunglings. Of course, such people had little chance of getting tenure, since their effectiveness came at the expense of published scholarship, and both found other jobs without waiting for the inevitable at Ohio State. The one-size-fits-all academic reward system is hardest of all on writing programs, and while I perhaps mitigated its worst effects here and there for a while, its myopia continues to distort the shape and stunt the accomplishment of every academic community.

6.

The excitement and stress of the job took a further toll on my already difficult relations with my children, especially my daughters Rachel and Linda, with whom these years produced deep rifts. Joan took Rachel to Latin America on her Guggenheim Fellowship for 1976-7, my first year as chairman. She was going to Chile to study its great poet Pablo Neruda, and on their way they spent a couple months in a Spanish language school in Mexico. Then the following spring Rachel got sick and came to live with me for three months while Joan finished out her year, during which she also helped a Chilean family escape Pinochet and emigrate to Seattle.

I sat up all night with Rachel for a week until she recovered, after which she became a bit testy with any single women I knew, including Robin. Yet the following summer, soon after Robin and I had moved into our new house, Rachel came for a visit during which she shyly asked to our complete surprise if she could come live with us permanently. I hemmed and hawed that this was perhaps possible but also had to be taken up with Joan in due time. But underneath that, Robin and I were both unnerved. Robin had always known she didn't want children, and at this stage neither did I. Not only was that an unspoken condition of our marriage, but the neighborhood we'd moved into was still in urban blight. The city's leading fence of stolen goods lived just around the block, and in those first years our house was broken into, there was an attempted rape next door, and frequent midnight collisions at the stoplight on our corner. Rachel was 13, the schools were problematic, and the courage she'd summoned to ask to live with us went for naught.

Then in September Joan was killed in a climbing accident in the Olympic Mountains. When her party had reached its destination and was ready to come down, she asked the leader if he'd be willing to take her further, which he did. But then on a scree slope he kicked loose a rock that bounced back and struck her in the forehead so that she could only say "Oh" before she was gone. Her body was flown out by helicopter two days later, and when I flew out to join her family and friends in mourning, Rachel would have nothing to do with me. I asked Joan's sister Margot and husband Tom to take her in with them and their children for a year while Robin and I got our feet on the ground. But after that year it was too late. Rachel wanted to finish high school at a private school with an equestrian program, which she could now afford with the money Joan had left her.

Her means now exceeded mine, and I resented the size of my support payments when she had inherited, besides an income from Joan's investments, Joan's Seattle house and the Boulder house we had bought together. For a while to my shame, this socialist charged his daughter for preparing her income tax. I think that for her this was the last straw, and, after three years and counting of unbroken pain when she'd needed me most, she felt abandoned emotionally and financially. She declined to apply to college at Ohio State as a faculty child and instead went to Mount Holyoke. Then for two years after graduating in 1987, she refused to visit, be visited, or accept money. Finally she came to feel there was no future in that, and we met at a restaurant in Northampton where, on the most terrible night of my life, Rachel told me all she'd been feeling and asked would I do the same things again if I had it all to do over. I replied through my tears without tasting my food that the one thing I'd still do is ask Margot and Tom to take her for that year. For the rest I asked forgiveness with a throbbing heart, and we've done a whole lot of healing since.

Robin and I got married in December, and then in the spring of 1979 Linda, now 26, moved from Berkeley to Columbus partly in the hope of reconnecting with me after years of feeling abandoned by both her parents. Not only had Bobby moved 2000 miles away, finally to Mendocino with its hippie culture in which Linda felt alien, but I had failed initially to contest Bobby for custody and then later to rescue Linda when I should have seen what was happening. Here in Columbus we had been close, and in my visits to Mendocino I had taken her prodigious gardening and art work as signs that she was thriving rather than desperately cultivating the only stability she could find.

Where Alex had gone away to a Quaker high school and made friends, Linda stayed in Mendocino at a makeshift school established by dropout parents, where she was the oldest and had to shepherd the younger ones. Then she moved to Berkeley, where she lived in a rooming house collective while getting a junior college degree and a secretarial job. Now she moved in with Robin and me for two months before finding an apartment, and over the next thirty years our healing has gone by fits and starts. She and Robin are often at odds, I feel caught in the middle, and, as if that weren't enough, Linda must struggle constantly with a daunting series of bio-neurological problems. She has all she can do to keep working successfully as a teacher, and while she has thought we don't understand why she can't just shape up, we have felt ignored after years of reaching out. All three of us keep on trying, and, with the help of advice and support from Alex and Rachel, lately we seem to be getting somewhere

7.

So it was that I found myself working to produce a new generation for our department without having been able to nurture my own children. One starting point is the hiring of new faculty, for whom the first prerequisite is a capacity for scholarly publication rather than democratic participation. In those years, hiring established scholars at senior ranks was extremely rare. Most of our hires were new Ph.D.'s, and we had a long tradition of hiring only people for whom a tenured position would be open following their probationary appointment. We knew the pain for everyone concerned when a person is denied tenure after six years, and our first concern was to make discriminating judgments of scholarly promise by reading in advance our applicants' writing and interviewing those whose work we liked best. Our questions in the interview could then probe not only a person's promise as scholar and teacher but also her capacity for contributing to our community. The working assumption was that we'd all be together for a long time, and this involved both a risk and an opportunity. The risk was that the career ambitions of a promising scholar could make her indifferent, or even hostile, to the common purpose and community we were trying to cultivate. The opportunity was that a promising scholar who was also committed to community might choose to remain with us for a professional lifetime.

Academics no more than others are equally versatile, and here at first I raised some hackles by insisting that our search committees be composed of people who were not only good judges of scholarship but also sharp questioners and listeners. Everybody wants her democratic "say" above all about hiring, and people vied for appointment to the search committees. But I was determined to use each according to her ability, and I did what I could to massage the egos of those with uneven abilities.

When my colleagues saw that pay off first of all in successful hires, they accepted this principle more readily for all our activities. It deepens the spirit of interdependence, just as with role-players in team sports, and along with it the community's capacity to reproduce itself. Of the six people we hired in my first year, it would have been very easy to overlook two, both of whom became exceptional not only as scholars and teachers but also as contributing citizens in our department. One was Jim Phelan, who, when he entered my hotel room to be interviewed, looked like he hadn't combed his hair in a week and was wearing a sports jacket and necktie for the first time in his life. He was not only nervous but visibly shy in sputtering out his answers to some seriously probing questions, and I doubt that any combination of more different interviewers than Jim Kincaid, Tom Mitchell, Chris Zacher, and myself could have identified this intellectual diamond in the sartorial rough.

The other was Lisa Kiser, who upon entering the room was as prepossessing in dress and manner as Jim Phelan was not. Her answers to our questions were smoothly forthcoming and revealed immediately a disciplined mind. Then, just when a couple of us began to suspect Lisa of being too glib to be true, she accompanied her answer to our final question on her dissertation by a wink and a half-smile: "Yes, you're right, and that will be the subject of my *second* book." In making the formulaic response appropriate to a ritual occasion, she could also risk mocking a professional culture to which she was deeply committed, and her playfulness here reassured us totally.

An interview team of sharp questioners and alert listeners is also attractive to the candidates you're most interested in, for whom Ohio State was then often at a competitive disadvantage. We couldn't afford not to make a good first impression, and in this regard it also helped for the chair to be active in the interview as *primum inter pares*. I had read the candidates' manuscripts, and (with a few exceptions) I didn't have to fake an interest in their work. My longtime cultivation of Socratic teaching had made me an effective interviewer, and I could speak honestly on behalf of my colleagues about the community we were trying to cultivate.

We made mistakes, of course; some people we hired didn't earn tenure, and some we didn't hire became famous somewhere else; some who earned tenure lost all further sense of purpose, and others' sense of purpose was narrowed to aggrandizing their personal careers. Even so, I believe our procedures succeeded in minimizing our fallibility while deepening our community. There was no budget then for bringing candidates to campus before making them offers, and I have yet to see evidence that the ostentatiously drawn out process of professional hiring to which my department has since turned, in what Henry James would surely call a "superstitious valuation" of participatory democracy, is more reliable than our practice back then. Now each of a dozen candidates for five or six positions makes a two- or three-day campus visit, costing thousands of dollars and untold faculty time devoted to hospitality (people recruited to "eat for the team" at a limit of $40 for food, $20 for wine, and a 20% tip per person per dinner at 2007 prices, but less for lunch), whose centerpiece is a "job talk." Here the candidate reads, to a random audience of those who might be free and so inclined at 4 p.m. on a weekday afternoon, a scholarly paper which the search committee has read before inviting her. When this paper is really good, as a good search committee knew it would be, or when it is mostly hot air because the search committee wasn't up to its job, everybody sees that and reacts accordingly. When it is somewhere in between, as it most often is, the discriminating judgment of a good search committee is no more likely to be ratified than the errant judgment of a bad one. But everybody has had her participatory say, and it has made no functional difference who was on the search committee.

I pushed to make our first-choice offers within two weeks of the interviews, so that we could impress the candidates with our promptness in recognizing their worth. Then came my annual tightrope dance. I explained to each person on the telephone that we didn't want her to respond to our offer before hearing from our competitors, but also that we didn't want to lose out on our second-choice candidates if she should turn us down. We needed to work together on this toward a good outcome for everyone. This transparency was evidently rare at that time, and it helped some candidates choose us. When they did, I involved myself directly in the logistics of their move. On one occasion, an Ohio State art historian couple wanted to sublet their apartment for a year, which was a perfect fit for our new Ph.D. couple moving sight unseen from Seattle. The trouble was for a bourgeois like me that art historians insist on painting their walls stark white and then scrupulously decline to hang anything on them. But when I apologized for this austerity to Steve Fink on the telephone, he didn't balk in the least, and I later discovered that among his several talents he is also an artist.

A second challenge to reproducing the peer community is the promotion and tenure process, and this one sapped my resiliency over the years. Here our recommendations to the university administration had to be approved first by a college committee advisory to the dean. This consisted of faculty from our sister departments chosen for their scholarly eminence, which often included a toxic combination of learned ignorance with supercilious arrogance taken on by self-anointed gatekeepers to the

Kingdom of Heaven. One year I proposed to my colleagues that we consider Gordon Grigsby for promotion to the rank full professor. They voted to consider him on the evidence available to be evaluated, and, after evaluating this evidence, voted to recommend him for promotion. Having published a couple of strong scholarly articles early on, Gordon had stopped doing scholarship and turned to writing poetry. Along the way he was the university's second winner of its Distinguished Teaching Award, and by now he was an established poet whose first collection, *Tornado Watch*, had earned wide praise because anyone with ears, mind, and heart for poetry has to be bowled over by an exceptional number of poems in this volume.

But I was hailed before the college committee to defend our recommendation, and the decisive question I was asked by an internationally renowned linguist was why Grigsby was not represented in Louis Untermeyer's anthology of modern poetry. Two years later I was again called before this committee (a weird honor in itself, since they didn't usually stoop that low) and asked to defend our recommendations that tenure and promotion be awarded to—Lisa Kiser and Jim Phelan. The questions I was asked about their splendid first books were as self-satisfiedly ignorant as Ilse Lehiste's about Gordon Grigsy's poetry, and this time I was really stunned. Our departmental vote on both candidates had been unanimous, as I remember, and I had tried to reflect the depth of our confidence in my letters transmitting the departmental recommendations. But where those letters were concerned, I was told by the dean that the college committee was suspicious of my prose. I went back to the office and wrote my resignation to have at the ready, then called him every few days for the two weeks it took him to reject his committee's advice.

There were also occasions when I felt I had to protect the department, not from its overseers but from itself, and one of these blighted my spirit still further. One of our own Ph.D.'s teaching writing at a satellite campus came up for his final decision on tenure and promotion, following an earlier decision that he must produce more publication or he wouldn't have a chance. I'd written him the required letter to this effect, and then added in conversation that I knew this wasn't likely to happen because of his workload in grading themes, but that we wanted to give him every conceivable opportunity. This was because we all loved Ken Rainey. He was a white Mississippian who, after risking everything he and his wife could do to advance the early civil rights struggle, had escaped North with their four children for Ken to attempt graduate school. His K-Mart blue jeans and dress shirts were always freshly washed and pressed, his melodious civility was an everyday pleasure, his academic record was ordinary, and in my graduate seminar on Dostoevsky and James he had surpassed himself with a brilliant term paper that I kept for decades and regularly pilfered in my teaching and writing.

When the time came at the meeting to discuss Ken's publication, it was as if everyone fell into a sudden amnesia and ignored the fact that his record was essentially unchanged from a year-and-a-half ago. If nothing else, it should have been obvious that any college committee would have no choice but to reject a positive recommendation, yet before I could collect my wits, my colleagues proceeded to vote that recommendation. I then whipped out and read them the letter I'd written Rainey last time about his needing to publish more, and I reminded all present that this message was from them and not me. A long silence followed, during which I began composing in my head still another resignation, until a motion to reverse the previous vote was shamefacedly carried and I was again off the hook.

The emotional wrench of this meeting was not only personal because I cared deeply for Ken Rainey. It was also profoundly political because, in protecting establishment values I was also protecting their injustice and hypocrisy that kept us from rewarding Rainey for doing what he had been hired to do. There was no chance we could make him the occasion of an academic revolution, and I thought we needed to preserve our credibility for battles we had a chance to win. Here is perhaps the boundary for a radical middle manager trying to maintain leverage inside the system, and working at this boundary was now becoming for me a gnawing expense of spirit.

Lisa Kiser, Jim Phelan, and Ken Rainey represented our younger generation, and behind them came our youngest, the graduate teaching assistants who aspired to the tenure-track jobs they had. TAs had long been regarded as professional apprentices with no political voice of their own, and even in some quarters as an institutional evil: Professor Tave of Chicago once described the graduate teaching assistantship in cold print as "the football scholarship of the learned clerks." Yet any number of scholars as accomplished even as Professor Tave owe their professional lives to the teaching assistantship, and some of these persist at football powerhouses like Ohio State. Following the 1970 strike, both our graduate and undergraduate students had been given a voice in departmental government, and now I did what I could to make their participation more functional. But the two big obstacles to incorporating graduate students in a departmental community are their transitory membership and their economic peonage—over which I experienced at last the crucifixion reflex I'd hoped all along to avoid.

Year after year in monthly meetings of department chairs with the dean, I was all but alone in trying to make increased TA stipends a college-wide issue. I argued that monies devoted to creating a mere show of scholarly *gravitas* on the chance of higher rankings in meaningless polls could be spent more in keeping with our humanistic values on increased TA stipends. But deans eager to rise in the administrative ranks, and department chairs eager to rise in the national rankings, were tone deaf to this argument, and I never got anywhere. Then in 1982, when their stipend increases had lagged behind inflation for consecutive years, TAs throughout the College of Humanities organized and threatened a strike. The ringleaders were of course from English, and our new dean appeared to suspect me of instigating them. He set up a radio command post in his office, from which he contacted me several times daily via walkie-talkie, as if to determine whether my troops were threatening his right flank or his left from across the street.

Not only had I nothing to do with this, but those TAs were not about to ask me or anyone else to fight their battles. So there I was, suspected on the one hand and ignored on the other, exquisitely caught in the martyr-making middle. I attended one of the TA meetings just to keep abreast of what was happening, and for an excruciating two minutes sitting in the back row, I felt a powerful impulse to raise my hand and come forward to bleed on the cross. I could hear myself saying, "I've been fighting for you all these years, and if you proceed in this way you won't get anywhere. But you've given me just the ammunition I need to succeed on your behalf, so calm down, be patient, and let me agonize to make this happen for you." But I managed to hold back, and they succeeded without my suffering any further. Along with increased stipends, they got an identity-shaping sense of political accomplishment.

8.

Another way the community reproduces itself is by cultivating new leadership among its existing members, and here I think I turned my personal insecurity into a strength. Peter Fleming says that we contribute to others from our own hurt, and beneath my public aplomb, my self-assurance is as uncertain as most people's. All the time I was chair I relied for advice not only on John Muste but also his successor vice-chairs, before whom I could think out loud and find direction in how to handle everything. In rehearsing my next moves while pacing their offices and puffing my cigars, I modeled my job for better and for worse, and I believe this deepened their confidence in deciding whether to continue in academic administration, and also their ability to succeed when they did.

When I'd asked John to step down as vice-chair, it was not so I could appoint any woman I could find. I had a person in mind, Marlene Longenecker, who blossomed like Pattie Dodd when given the opportunity. Marlene was a beloved and honored teacher, and now her quick mastery as vice-chair led in two years to her appointment as chair of our Women's Studies program at a time when its future hinged on the outcome of a rift between lesbian and straight faculty. Over the next six years her diplomacy, firmness, and caring healed this rift, and our Women's Studies department became one of the most admired in the country. She was then appointed press secretary to the Ohio governor's wife, took a leave of absence from the university, and, upon returning to the English department with her breadth of experience, became one of its prolific wise elders.

Marlene was not only a feminist but also a broad-gauge radical like me: in the 70s she'd interrupted graduate school to live for two years in a commune, then got a Ph.D from SUNY-Buffalo when its English department was full of mavericks like Lionel

Abel and Leslie Fiedler. Now I was intent that her successor should not be of our political ilk but should reflect the department's diversity, and David Frantz also turned out to be a serendipitous choice. Like Marlene, David was a prize-winning teacher, and now he flourished in administration just as she had. But where she had worn tie-dyed, ankle-length dresses with sandals, he wore oxford cloth shirts with foulards and tweeds. His father had been a headmaster, his B.A .was from Princeton and his Ph.D. from Penn, and he was the poker game's consummate bluffer. Yet underlying all their differences in sensibility and style, Marlene and David share a problem-solving civility informed by their commitment to liberal education. And where she brought the power of this commitment into Women's Studies and the governor's office, he later brought it to a long series of university positions, finally as secretary to our Board of Trustees, where with fine-tuned diplomacy he kept people focused on the educational purpose that is our reason for being.

9.

The dean who finally came through for our teaching assistants was Diether Haenicke, an urbane professor of German and sporadic humanist who, when he calmed down enough to see what was minimally just, turned off his walkie-talkie and did the right thing. Art Adams had left the deanship after my first year, and after a year's interim with an acting dean, Diether was hired away from Wayne State where he'd been provost. He and I got off immediately on the wrong foot: I didn't take time at first to feel him out by moderating the no-minced-words forthrightness that was habitual with Adams, and after one of our early encounters, in which I resisted his hidebound thinking on the problem at hand, Diether didn't talk to me for a month. Then I took him to lunch, we cleared the air and became warm friends, respecting each other's minds and enjoying each other's conversation, up to a point. For as far as I could tell, all his new friendships at that time were constrained by his professional ambition.

He had not left the provost's job at Wayne State only to remain a dean at Ohio State, and in due course he indeed became our provost. But then he was passed over for our presidency and had to settle for the presidency of a third-tier university. While following this trajectory to ultimate disappointment, Diether always seemed to feel it his duty to make everyone shape up, especially us in English with our participatory fervor and political *amour propre*, in response to his micro-management. Unlike Mike Tomlin upon becoming coach of the Pittsburgh Steelers and announcing he wouldn't impose his 4-3 defense on a team built for the 3-4, Diether came in swinging a machete. I kept quiet and swallowed hard when he ordered that our spacious and sun-lit secretarial space be fitted with cubicle partitions so as to keep the secretaries from socializing with the faculty or each other. But of course he didn't stop there, and the time came when I was ready once again to tender my resignation.

Salary raises were for me sacred territory to defend on behalf of the principle of peer review in a democratic workplace. In those days before universities had succumbed to the fiction of a free market in people, each year's raise money was divided between "across the board" (aka cost of living) and "merit." The percentage to be allotted for across the board was decided by university administrators behind closed doors, but the allotment itself was based on the principle that everybody should have some before anybody gets more. The merit raise was decided by the departments, and while in some departments this meant the chair acting alone (or with advice from two cronies), in English it had been decided for decades through a half-socialist process of peer review. In the socialist half, we discussed each other's contributions to the department's work and mission, and we voted to designate individuals as priorities for raises, leaving exact amounts to the chair. In the feudal half, the associate and full professors voted on the assistant professors' raises, the full professors on the associate professor's raises, and the full professors individually with the chair on each other's raises. All our recommendations were then subject to negotiation with the dean, whose occasional veto still left intact a peer evaluation process.

Within this process the chair had some room for maneuver, and I tried to use mine to overcome by sly annual increments what seemed to me inequities—between good scholars and good teachers; between thinking scholars and make-work scholars; between less contributing people who'd got big across the board

136

increases in good budget years and more contributing people who'd missed out on those years. I had also learned from Bob Estrich the tactic of "leap-frogging" merit raises—one year recommending X for a big raise for having published an important book, and the next year recommending Y to overtake X for having a better cumulative record. It was all tricky business, but most people recognized the essential fairness over time of our salary profile.

But one year Diether decided we had gone socialistically too far in not giving a bigger raise to a professor who had just won a national prize. He warned me in advance of our budget meeting that he'd want to discuss all our recommendations in detail, and, anticipating a tense meeting, I asked David Frantz to come along and hold my hand. Raises were then awarded in multiples of $12, and, sure enough, Diether seemed ready to challenge every $12 we had allocated to every member of a faculty of 65. But the person he kept coming back to was our Harvardian Stanley Kahrl, whose exotic specialty was medieval drama and whose baker's dozen of colleagues from across the land had voted him this prize—not for any particular work of scholarship but for his long-term contribution to their field. Grateful as we were for Kahrl's citizenship in our department, neither my colleagues nor I thought this prize a great achievement: many networks of specialists circulate prizes among themselves. I reminded Diether of this, and I also explained our good reasons for recommending others ahead of Kahrl. But he was adamant, and after two hours we sat glowering at each other in silence for five minutes that felt like another hour. I began composing a resignation in my head, and then to my astonishment Diether broke the silence by going completely overboard in the opposite direction. David reminds me that his words were, "Julian, you know I won't deny you, so let's go with all your recommendations." After apparently satisfying himself with a show of toughness, he came through here just as he had for the TAs with their stipends.

Responding to periodic budget crises was a whole other story. Here the department chair is called on to protect as much of her budget as she can by tactically outmaneuvering her overlords. When the legislature's allocation was substantially less than expected, the invariable first reflex of provosts and deans was to rattle their fiefs' cages by declaring an emergency. I didn't take these declarations too seriously, since I had long ago come to see how much budget fat can be trimmed without compromising any pedagogical or scholarly use-value. Nor do I remember any crisis materializing on the scale we'd been told to expect. But there were periodic hiring freezes, along with required plans to trim our budgets by a hypothetical 2%, 5%, or 10%, and one of these wore down my stamina yet further. This was a hiring freeze imposed not by the university but only by Diether Haenicke for the College of Humanities, and only after I had made telephone offers to our first-choice candidates by way of wishing them Happy New Year for 1982. I had explained as always that a written letter of offer was forthcoming but that we wanted them to know our decision as soon as it was made. Then Diether told me to inform them that nothing was in writing and all bets were off. Knowing him as I now did, I felt certain that this was just another reflex gesture. But by that time the job market had entered its long-term contraction that made our offers newly attractive, and several of our candidates had turned down other offers on the strength of my now discredited word. Now I could only ask them to hold their breath on the tremulous strength of my further word that the freeze would be quickly lifted. We were all near our wits end, and one splendid young Shakespearean decided then and there not to endure this profession any longer but instead go to law school. The others hung in for thirty-six hours until Diether lifted the freeze and redeemed my gamble.

10.

While we were interviewing that Shakespearean in my Manhattan hotel room during the week after Christmas in 1981, I got a call from my sister Mimi telling me our mother just died, and I excused myself from the interview to take a walk outdoors in my first wave of grief. Fritzie was now 88, and in my last Chicago visits to the nursing home where she lived, I had taken my turn at changing her diaper before walking her step by step to a Chinese restaurant two blocks away. Her memory was gone, and almost all that was left was her sourness. Walking now through Manhattan's frigid midtown streets, I felt sharply again the pain, shame, and guilt of my fights with her, and then I was flooded by memories of my mother's love of life.

After school in winter as a young girl, she'd hitchhiked rides on farmers' sleighs to the Carnegie Library in Goshen, where she raised the librarians' eyebrows by reading not only Shakespeare's plays but also Balzac's novels. Any number of books on our family shelves were inscribed with her maiden name, and those with my father's were mostly in her handwriting. At her first job in Chicago she made herself indispensable as a legal stenographer, and after getting married she took sewing classes while also teaching herself to cook. My father Al was all thumbs with a hammer or screwdriver, so Fritzie became the family handywoman until I grew up and took over. When a small oil fire began under our 1928 Graham Paige in the garage after my dad hit the starter, he ran upstairs to our apartment to call the fire department, and, while he was on the phone, she filled a scrub bucket with water, ran downstairs, and put out the fire. The fire truck arrived with blaring sirens and half the neighborhood in tow, and my poor dad had to explain while my mom was all smiles.

She fell in love with the postwar Broadway musical—*Oklahoma, Finian's Rainbow, My Fair Lady*. She'd see the Chicago road company performance, then buy the recording and waltz to it around the living room with flailing arms. While dancing with me she was jerky, but she was lost in the music and absolutely didn't care. She wore out her recording of Paul Robeson's *Othello*, and long before anyone outside Chicago had heard of Studs Terkel, she was his devoted radio listener. In her ladies' bridge club she was the one dealt those awful nine-point hands, with which she often proceeded to set a three-no-trump bid while thoughtfully sipping her Miller High Life beer.

After my dad died and I was married, my mother was at loggerheads with my wild adolescent sister, so she got a job as a sorority housemother in Oklahoma while Mimi stayed in Chicago to go to Roosevelt College. A couple of years later she came back and enrolled alongside Mimi at Roosevelt, where she became research assistant to Professor Weinberg in Sociology and copy-edited his book manuscripts. That ended when she got a call from the big-time lawyer she'd worked for when she first came to

Chicago, and now she returned to Mr. Jacobson as His Girl Friday forty years later. Meanwhile she had an autumnal affair with Jack Zalkind, the dashing, bow-tied lawyer she'd had her eye on before Al proposed to her, and who had remained a bachelor all those years.

So here is my understanding of my mother's life as a contradiction that was sustained only at the expense of sporadic depression and sourness. Her flow of curiosity, intelligence, and purpose would have made her in my generation a lawyer or professor like her husband and sons. Her subjection as a woman in her generation, even in what was then an enlightened marriage, could only frustrate her the more for having to disperse and stunt the use of her talents. Yet for all but a few of her 88 years, Frieda Wolfberg overreached her depression and refused to lead a disappointed life. I knew by now how much I was her son both for better and for worse, and in the pain of reaching this knowledge I had been very hard on her. But I had also been her bridge partner, her dance partner for *My Fair Lady,* her deep-structure political heir. Nor can I ever thank her enough for the range of books and ideas she opened to me while exploring for herself the possibilities of human life.

11.

By the beginning of the 1982-3 academic year I could feel myself burning out, and, after talking it over with Robin, I wrote the dean that I'd like to cut my second term short and leave the job at the end of that year. Looking back now on my seven years, I can't see them as publicly memorable. The English department had not become a larger presence in the university, and its national reputation had improved modestly if at all. In literary and cultural studies, the new theoretical "isms" of that era were initiated at Berkeley, Hopkins, Irvine, and Yale, and, like most others, Ohio State had played catch-up beneath the professional radar. Nor had I anything to do with the continuing flow of useful scholarship and serious thought that my colleagues went on producing in the work of Richard D. Altick, James Battersby, Walter A. Davis, John B. Gabel & Charles B. Wheeler, Lisa Kiser, and Jim Phelan (to name only those). Even so, the sense of accomplishment I came away with was mostly what I'd hoped for when I sat trembling at the outset. With the support of many colleagues, I had helped my department enlarge its intellectual horizons while also becoming a more vibrant community. We had deepened the ambience in which our sense of common purpose was clear, our democracy productive, and our morale nourishing to most of us one by one. That is what people thanked me for at the end, and I've carried it with me.

Over the ensuing years I've observed from the list-serve sidelines how much more difficult the chair's job has become in the twenty-first century corporate university—or, perhaps, just how much harder it would be now to try what I tried. The culture and accomplishment of the peer community are now subject more than ever to erosion by the commoditized culture of university administrators whose priority is to increase market share of factitious prestige without incurring lawsuits. In today's university where publicists, fundraisers, auditors, and lawyers reach their tentacles into every corner of academic life, so that the faculty must serve them instead of the other way around, I would not have got past square one as a department chair. Thus do I stand the more in awe of my department's recent chair, Valerie Lee, whose Ph. D. dissertation I directed way back when, and who now worked her way through each day's e-mail with an alertness, transparency, intelligence, and wit that sustained the morale of a department perhaps more congenial than the one I left. As I said in a fan letter I once e-mailed her (and hope she might have read), when I became chair I took Bob Estrich as my role model, but if I were young and crazy enough to attempt it thirty years later, my model would be Valerie her own self.

CHAPTER 6. POLITICAL PRACTICE AND THEORETICAL REFLECTION:

COLUMBUS, 1983-2003

Over the eight years between my leaving the department chair and retiring from the university, I found myself shrinking in some ways and expanding in others. My excitement in the classroom began to fade, while my experience in service had now put me in a position, as a basketball coach would say, to let the game come to me. In the university I was offered service assignments whose political dynamics challenged me in ways the classroom no longer did, and I also became active in the community by joining a handful of others to save Columbus's public market. These experiences exposed me to the underside of politics in the university and the city, and reflecting on all that afterwards while reading in retirement centered my marxism more firmly than ever.

Once retired, I published a tentative article articulating this marxism, and this one led to another and then another, until I saw how to make a book that became *The Marxian Imagination*. This is a work of literary criticism and theory, but its argument is grounded in what I'd seen of the community where I live, and I believe this argument still needs to be reckoned with. So it turned out at last that my teaching and service converged in my scholarship and made me (in my eyes) the kind of scholar-thinker I'd hoped to become when I first started out.

I was in post-partum depression for six months after leaving the department chair, and I've understood since how hard it is for professional athletes to retire even when their bodies tell them it's time. In those years as chair my spirit had been nourished by feelings of accomplishment in doing something I was good at, and I'd also been a privileged insider to high level decision-making and gossip. Now I was out of all the loops and back in the classroom practicing my first love, yet without quite the pizzazz of those early days when I was finding my way as a teacher. Now, every time I walked past the dean's conference room, I felt a pang of regret. Yet leaving the chairmanship was also a rehearsal in letting go, and by the time I retired I was freshly excited by the re-thought marxism I was then discovering. Instead of going into relapse I could pursue new intellectual adventures, and that made retirement when it came feel something like liberation.

In the classroom I tried to freshen my teaching by devising new courses (e.g., "The Literature of Oppression") and by varying still further the readings in my old standby courses. But none of that brought back the old edge. I was aware as never before how undergraduates are perpetually nineteen years old, and graduate students not quite my equals no matter how much I might treat them so. Not that I now stinted on my teaching, and in student evaluations I was praised as before for my knowledge, organization, and caring. But I had also become more coolly Olympian and less restlessly provocative, for no matter what topic we took up in the classroom, I saw all too soon where the process was taking us, and I had a growing sense of diminishing returns on what I could learn in this process.

One reason for that, as it now seems to me, was the new generation of students. Unlike those of the 70s, many of whom couldn't wait to pick up on your questions and run with them, too many of these students seemed inert until you jolted them with a quiz. Then the best ones responded very much as in the 70s, but now as the 80s wore on, I sensed a growing number sitting in that classroom just daring me to entertain them without engaging their minds. More than ever, they seemed to me to be in college simply to improve their earning power, and well on their way to becoming the X-generation's passively recalcitrant consumers of education.

I had also reached a limit on how much more I wanted to read in working with graduate students. Besides preparing and teaching my classes through the years, I had directed some two dozen Ph.D. dissertations, and many M.A. theses, on a spectrum of topics ranging from the theory of Shakespearean comedy to the American *bildungsroman*, the novels of George Lippard and of F. Scott Fitzgerald, the male/female double in women's fiction, melodrama in Henry James, and the Zoroastrian mystical number

"3" in *Moby-Dick* (the *Pequod* 's three masts, three mates, three harpooners, three days' chase of the great whale, all just for openers.) Not only had I done the reading entailed by this range of topics, but also the grunt work of getting mentally inside my students' arguments to help strengthen their logic and coherence, and then filter their prose to make it more efficient and plainspoken.

I had also formed friendships with some wonderful graduate students—Carol Bowles, Steve Busonik, Woo Yong Chun, Martina Ebert, Arnold Hartstein, Nan Nowik, Susan Yadlon, and my beloved Malcolm Griffith. But now I balked at taking up all that work again on topics unrelated to the marxism I was finding new occasions to re-think. Nor could I attract graduate students into exploring this marxism with me. On the rare occasions when it might be relevant to introduce it in class, they listened politely, but their minds were already co-opted by some other –ism prevailing at the moment—structuralism, post-modernism, post-colonialism—all of which declare themselves emphatically post-marxist no matter how they might differ from one another. And so it was that for the very first time, I found myself declining to direct dissertations by students whose work I admired quite apart from their topics.

2.

I was meanwhile being appointed to select university committees, including two that were concerned with affirmative action for African-Americans, and my experience on these committees put an end to my acceptance of identity politics. Despite Ohio State's long record of graduating more black Ph.D.'s than any university in the country, and despite its strong Black Studies Program, we were still not admitting African-American undergraduates in anything like their proportion of the population, and among those we did admit, an embarrassingly small fraction went on to graduate. An earlier report on this problem had been gathering dust on the shelf, and now President Jennings asked us to make a new effort to formulate a university-wide policy of affirmative action—recruiting and retaining African-American students, faculty, and staff.

In fact, he asked something like twenty of us, because on so sensitive a subject every identity category had to be represented on the committee—African-Americans, women, and two white males; students, faculty, and administrators; the departments of social work, astronomy, and athletics—everybody except the janitors and food workers who acquired no identity from their daily labor in keeping the whole place going on behalf of the rest of us. Our numbers made this the most unwieldy committee I was ever a part of, and, if not for our general intelligence and good will, along with the skill of our chairperson, I doubt we would have got off the ground. Mari Jones was a tough-minded professor of psychology who proved adept at sorting out the issues and moving the discussion forward, and I did my part by volunteering to write the multiple drafts of our final report.

We made a series of recommendations, running from the personal recruiting of African-American students from inner-city schools to cutting the budgets of university departments that regularly failed to hire African-Americans when these were well represented among the candidates. But my lasting memory is not of this report but of a fellow committee member, Phyllis Bailey, Ohio State's long-time associate director of athletics responsible for women's sports. She and I were later to become friends, but my first reaction to this total stranger was simple amazement that a person from the Department of Athletics could be so smart and articulate. It didn't hurt that Phyllis stands over six feet tall and has a richly resonant voice. Yet in this company that wouldn't have mattered if what she had to say weren't so incisive, timely, and distilled from hands-on experience. From Day One it was clear that when Phyllis spoke everybody would listen, especially because she would say it only once, right to the point.

Beneath the radar of an all-male athletic department whose showpiece was championship football, Phyllis Bailey for three decades had been negotiating budget to add women's teams, hire coaches, elevate the quality of play, and provide women athletes with counseling support equivalent to that of men. She has never been an avowed feminist, and I suspect that her 2008 presidential vote for Barack Obama was the first in her life for a Democrat. But when the NCAA's "Title IX" was promulgated in 1972 in support of women's equal opportunity to participate in intercollegiate athletics, Ohio State was the rare institution that didn't need to scurry in order to catch up. The nationwide whining about having to abolish men's teams in order to add women's was irrelevant to us. So our committee of scholars had something to learn from this one-time basketball coach, and our report included recommendations both for recruiting black students and then for supporting them once they were here.

Yet almost in the next institutional breath, these recommendations had to be reconciled with those of a subsequent university committee on Selective Admission. Just like women's sports, the university itself had been growing in accomplishment and stature under the national radar. We were increasingly prolific in research and deep in curriculum, and our proportion of honors student applicants was increasing with each year's freshman class. One perceived drag on our further development was our long-standing first-come, first-serve, open admissions policy for every Ohio high school graduate. Not only honors students but all others were now applying in greater numbers, and we had intensified our recruitment of minorities. With this growing flood of applicants, first-come, first-serve was no longer a viable method of selection, since all it could do was advance the application deadline beyond reason, and the question became, what could be? What criteria for admission could we devise so as to offer something like equal justice to both precocious honors students and disadvantaged African-Americans?

The Committee on Selective Admission, whose first chair was another tough-minded woman, Professor Betty Menaghan of Sociology, spent its first year doing exhaustive research on this question. They read studies of the high school predictors of success and the effectiveness of college support programs; they did their own statistical analyses and tested their mysterious algorithms; and by the end of that year they proposed an interlocking set of differentially weighted criteria for admission to Ohio State. Not SAT scores but high school class rank (adjusted for the high school's performance record) was found to be the most reliable predictor of success in college, and they weighted this one most heavily. Then came such things as difficulty of high school courses taken, special talents for the arts or athletics, special hardships, minority status, and, finally, SAT scores.

I was appointed chair of this committee for its second year, during which our task was to fine-tune the model and present it for adoption. And now in the 80s, as if nothing had changed since the Black Power 60s, our entire project was condemned as racist by what had meanwhile become the university's Black Establishment. Following the 1970 strike, Ohio State had recruited African-Americans into every level of university administration, including deanships and the vice-presidency for minority affairs, whose now long-time incumbent was a veteran civil rights activist. African-Americans were of course well represented on our committee, and they had participated fully in the deliberative process that brought us to where we were now. Yet a member of the committee felt obliged at the last minute to go behind this process by informing Vice-President Hale of our next meeting, and when he phoned me to request that he be allowed to attend, I replied that our meetings were open and he would always be welcome.

I learned later that Hale had been kept officially informed of our predecessors' work leading up to this meeting, but I knew nothing about that at the time, and when he now arrived at the meeting with an African-American delegation larger than our committee and tried in effect to pre-empt us with a sit-in, I was taken wholly off guard. After two confrontational exchanges, I saw this could only lead to a stand-off, and I fell back by reflex on my experience as department chair. I announced we would proceed to our agenda, copies of which I distributed to our visitors; I promised to recognize anyone who wished to speak about any item on this agenda; and I insisted that nobody speak until recognized. A tense silence followed, during which I thought things might go either way, and after a short interval I took silence for consent, thanked my lucky stars, and proceeded to this agenda. Since our visitors had given little thought to the actual criteria we were considering, the committee was soon on top of its own meeting and pursuing its deliberations for all to see and hear. And once Frank Hale had been faced down, some of his people were ready to listen.

The long-term results of Ohio State's Selective Admission policy are an increasingly accomplished entering class, of which a stable cohort are African-Americans still far smaller than their proportion of the population, and along with this a steadily improving graduation rate for everyone black and white. I suppose it can still be argued that the policy is racist insofar as it produces a freshman class whose minorities are under-represented without reason because the class as a whole is overqualified for our curriculum. But that would also be an argument for limiting the curriculum in deference to minorities, and I can't see that as a victory over racism. As far as I was concerned, Frank Hale had lapsed into tunnel vision since his days in the civil rights movement, and this experience put an end to my acceptance of the identity politics through which I'd been expelled from that movement all those years ago.

My participation in black struggle began inadvertently on Chicago's packinghouse picket line in 1948. Those packinghouse workers, who happened coincidentally (!) to be black, were not striking for civil rights or the identity conferred by these rights, but simply for a decent wage, which they didn't get then and haven't got since. I had then gone on, like my sister Mimi and my brother Chuck and millions of others, to participate in a civil rights movement that transformed America to the point where we could elect as president an African-American whose intelligence, compassion, and eloquence put his predecessor to shame. But this electoral triumph of identity has left virtually untouched those packinghouse workers' millions of heirs, black, brown, and white, who remain prime candidates for selective admission to unemployment lines, homeless shelters, and prisons.. And nothing within the scholarly capacity of today's universities with their identity-curricula—African-American Studies, Gay & Lesbian Studies, Native American Studies, Women's Studies—enables them morally or methodologically to address this phenomenon.

So it happened that in retirement some fifty years after walking that stockyards picket line, I walked another one in early dawn at Gate 23 to Ohio State's football stadium. The university was then spending millions to renovate "The Horseshoe" at a time when its janitors, cafeteria workers, and hospital orderlies were on strike for the same real wage they'd had thirty years earlier. The construction workers arriving at Gate 23 in their pickup trucks were overwhelmingly high-wage white males, while the food workers on the picket line singing in their sandals were overwhelmingly low-wage black females. They persuaded those men to honor their picket and go home for the day, which cost the university some serious money and embarrassment. That encouraged it to soften its previous intransigence with a cosmetic wage increase which the strikers decided they had no choice but to accept.

3.

In the first years of our marriage Robin and I had no money for vacations, and we'd spend a week each summer in Ocean City, MD, with its year-round population of 40,000 and then 250,000 in the summer, where her sister Tracy worked as a single mother in the hospitality industry. When their mother died in 1990, their father moved to Ocean City, and we kept returning after we started vacationing elsewhere. Once we could afford that, I introduced Robin to mountain hiking, which she took to immediately, and we kept going to America's national parks rather than European cities and museums. Robin is in many ways the same sort of hiker I am, less invested in the summit than in the rhythm of reaching it. But also beyond that, she is an informed naturalist, which I am not, and she is endlessly excited by the changing contours, flora, fauna, and light of different locales and elevations—the cactus fields of New Mexico, the east face of Long's Peak, the mountain goats of Montana, the light above Taos, the humming birds of west Texas, the wildflowers blooming everywhere along the trails below tree-line.

When we got out of the car for our first climb together up Santa Fe Baldy (which I had previously climbed alone), Robin the born alarmist asked if there were snakes. I said no, only sometimes around the parking lot, and none here this morning. Twenty minutes later, just as we were getting into our rhythm, a rattlesnake crossed the trail ahead of us while going about its business, and at the end of the day when we pitched our tent at Williams Lake just beneath the summit, she made me scour the campsite for half an hour before taking off her backpack.

We hiked in Sequoia National Park while visiting my son Alex, in Rocky Mountain National Park while visiting the Kincaids, in Big Bend, Grand Canyon, Zion, and others. We went once to the Swiss Alps, where we moseyed around beneath the

Matterhorn and in the Berner Oberland I was so slow crossing a snowfield at dusk that we almost missed the last gondola down. But the place we kept coming back to, on foot and in our hearts, was Glacier National Park. We have been there four times, and while no serious mountaineer would condescend to climb its peaks, their soft majesty and light are magical, and I sometimes think of having my ashes dropped there. Once on what the trail guide listed as an 11-mile round trip, we were overtaken below the summit ridge by two young guys who assured us it would be just a few extra steps to go over the top and loop back around on the other side. We were still pretty fresh, and saturated in spirit by this wondrous place from two days already of hiking. So we went for it, and up on that ridge a fierce snow storm blew up and shredded Robin's poncho right off her back. Then it turned out that the loop those guys sold us made it a 17-mile, totally zoned-in day, which I wouldn't have traded for anything.

I didn't hike in the mountains for the sake of learning lessons in marxism but just for the joy of doing it. Yet it turned out that all this hiking, like the years of teaching and service, fed into my marxism upon further reflection. When you exert all your strength to maintain contact with an indifferent Earth in its overwhelming silence everywhere you hike, you can also come to see this Earth as a textbook in un-intelligent design—a showplace of wonders like the Grand Canyon and the human eye, a gallery of grotesques like the anteater and the booby, and a chaos of conflicting processes like tectonic shift and the dinosaur extinction—from which, among other things, the descent of man could not have been predicted. It took Darwin and his heirs heroic effort to sort out the tangle of our terrestrial history—geological cataclysms, life's false starts, dead ends, crossroads accidents, and improbable survivors—so that we can now see in hindsight the master narrative that explains how we got here. And the research methodology that makes this narrative compelling is what Marx called historical materialism. In reading Darwin, Ernst Mayr, Stephen Jay Gould, Richard Levins & R.W. Lewontin, I was soon to see an army of scholars searching throughout earthly space in order to assemble their taxonomies of silts, fossils, creatures, and processes, and then only make sense of this chaos in space by figuring out its logic of process in time. For almost two centuries they have been following the slogan lately coined by the marxist Fredric Jameson (a slogan my old teacher Henry Smith would have loved), "Always historicize!"

Marx was an early admirer of Darwin, writing to LaSalle in 1860 that "Darwin's book ...serves me as a basis in natural science for the class struggle in history," and marxists historicize the ascent of humans in much the same way as evolutionists our descent. Once established as a species, we have kept on enlarging what Marx called our "species being" and, in so doing, produced our own vast geography of false starts and dead ends, golden ages and terrible holocausts, fateful coincidences and unlikely survivors. Our social evolution, like our physical, could have been cut off at many points along the way, and that might happen yet. But meanwhile it exhibits its own logic of process in the master narrative of human progress from slavery through feudalism to capitalism (and, if we're lucky, socialism), in a sequence that could no more have been reversed than Mesozoic, Paleozoic, Precambrian, and Cambrian. And just as our species might not have got here, unbeknownst to ourselves, without the Cambrian explosion, we might also prove unable to remain without adopting in full knowledge the morality of socialism. I arrived at this understanding by reading books, of course, but I had also been prepared for it by walking our Earth in its vast confusion of meaningless and meaningful material forms.

4.

I was also stimulated to further marxian reflection by two political experiences during the late 80s and early 90s, one in the university and one in the city, which exposed me to a more tremulous interplay of human circumstance, purpose, and accident than any I had seen yet. The university is not an ivory tower detached from "the real world" but an integral a part of this world, just like General Motors or the National Football League. Yet also like them, it is an institutional cocoon whose internal politics are more circumscribed and predictable than those of the community at large. I now had some authority in the academic politics whose traditions can sometimes be accommodating to my socialist impulses. But that didn't qualify me for the street politics of the wider community, which are all that many people know and to which I was now introduced.

In the year before I retired, the university provost offered me a three-month troubleshooting assignment, which I accepted because the added salary for those months would also increase my pension. Like many states, during the 60s Ohio had established a network of two-year satellite campuses to its public universities. The idea was to bring the first two years of college within commuting distance of every student in the state, from which she could then proceed to a four-year campus if things worked out. Each regional campus included a technical institute alongside its arts and sciences program, and there was often competition between these two for salaries, office space, budget, and status.

Lima was Ohio State's largest regional campus, and its newly appointed dean was a low-order mathematician with deeper affinities for the technical institute, and local Kiwanis Club, than for the liberal arts and sciences. The deeply flawed search process by which he was chosen had somehow gone unnoticed by the university administration, and now some of Lima's arts and sciences faculty were petitioning the university provost for redress of grievances. The provost worried from his distance that these petitioners might just be whining, and he sought advice for sending a fair-minded person to Lima in order to investigate the situation objectively. Irony of ironies! he was advised to send me, the boilerplate English department leftist—and, as if that weren't enough, when I got there I discovered that the rebel faculty leader was not a rabble-rousing comrade from English but a shy, soft-spoken, politically innocent professor of Greek and Latin.

During my years as department chair I had regularly visited the regional campuses, and I had come to admire the Lima faculty for the devotion and quality of both its teaching and research. A number of these people, in the sciences as well as the humanities, were producing scholarship comparable to that of their Columbus colleagues, and when as department chair I'd instituted exchange teaching with regional campus faculty, our Columbus students certainly had not suffered in the classroom. So while I now doubted these faculty were just whining, I was also determined to follow the evidence like any TV crime scene investigator.

For ten weeks I spent four days a week in Lima, where from my cubicle office in the campus library I established regular contact with the dean and his critics, while also inviting to come see me anyone who felt she could shed light on the situation. The two main grievances of James Countryman's critics were that he valued community service out of all proportion to teaching and research, and that he was a political autocrat who couldn't tolerate democratic decision-making by the faculty. As my old boss Art Adams might have said on their behalf, in this dean's domain everything was feudalism.

From my weekly conversations with Countryman, on which I took notes while facing him directly, it became clear how all this might be so. He didn't even bother paying lip-service to the customary platitudes about education for citizenship and the value of the liberal arts, and he seemed to regard faculty research that produced salary raises as an unfortunate diversion of budget from the campus's mission to the Lima community. His condescension toward teaching and scholarship in the arts and sciences was unmistakable, and so was his impatience with the faculty's desire to have a voice in its own government.

As if that weren't enough, over those weeks a variety of people contacted me furtively to complain about this man. Once it was known who I was and why I was there, his avowed critics promptly came forward, while his supporters, most of them associated with the technical institute, boycotted me on what they seemed to think the safe assumption that my investigation wouldn't be credible without their cooperation. But as time went on, first one person and then another came out of the woodwork. A woman phoned to ask if I would meet her after hours at a Pizza Hut off campus, in whose pepperoni fumes she identified herself as a secretary whom Countryman (she said) had humiliated repeatedly in public with his sexist sarcasms and put-downs. A janitor just happened to run into me behind the building where he worked and told me he was arbitrarily subject to cleaning and repair assignments beyond his job description and daily schedule. Two low-level faculty in the technical institute apologized for waiting this long to come see me because they feared for their jobs, but now had decided they couldn't let all this pass without bearing witness to Countryman's arbitrary rule.

The growing buzz during these weeks also affected people of good will who felt no grievance and had ignored the controversy. A smart and accomplished woman who worked directly for Countryman questioned me periodically about what I was learning and became increasingly pained to see how the shoe might fit. With her as with others, I was careful not to divulge my sources but simply to summarize what I was hearing, and a time came when Countryman's supporters realized their boycott wasn't working. At the next-to-last minute they too sought me out, some quite angrily, and their two arguments on his behalf were that he had established strong relations with the Lima community and that his critics were just whiners. My final report endorsed their first argument that close town and gown relations are central to the university's land-grant mission. But it also countered their second argument by quoting Countryman against himself, and that was enough to get him fired.

All of this added up for me to a poignant cultural phenomenon. Like many small Midwestern cities, Lima had once had grand hopes and pretensions. Railroad engines were once built here, and now roller bearings were almost the only thing left. More industry had disappeared than remained, and, as a Lima campus trustee wistfully told me while trying to call me off, "Every young person in Lima with any get-up-and-go has got up and gone." The Ohio State campus provided not only local jobs but also a psychological buffer to the city's fading economy and feeling of community.

The trouble was that a land-grant university is an intellectual as well as a vocational institution, and, as the historian Richard Hofstadter famously showed, our national history is steeped in anti-intellectualism. Insofar as Lima's liberal arts faculty might grace the campus with art exhibits, science fairs, or theatrical performances, the community could welcome it warmly. But insofar as its daily teaching and research were broadly scientific and cultural rather than narrowly vocational, the community could feel uneasily remote and perhaps a bit suspicious. Where the technical institute prepared students for local blue-collar jobs familiar to their parents, the liberal arts program led them to B.A. degrees earned away from home to give them white-collar earning power through a mysterious symbolism. These were most likely the kids who had got up and gone, and that might have had something to do with their study of science and history, sociology and politics, literature and philosophy.

The land-grant ideal of continuity between the mechanic and liberal arts, in which practical know-how, conceptual analysis, and civic purpose are seamlessly joined, has often been vindicated in episodes of American history where our technological pursuits were governed by the social and ethical standards embodied by the liberal arts. But this symbiosis of technological problem-solving with civic purpose can also make Americans uneasy because their livelihoods under capitalism often depend on its absence. They work in an economy that must grow at all costs, including moral and social costs, and they may sense very well how material growth for its own sake is incompatible with the citizenship taught by the liberal arts. The situation at Lima was for me a reflection of America's land-grant dilemma under capitalism.

5.

Still during my Lima sojourn, I joined with others in a strenuous, protracted, and accidentally successful effort to save Columbus's last surviving public market. In our first years there back in the 1950s, Bobby and I took the kids on Saturdays to the outdoor Central Market covering a four-block stretch through the middle of downtown. Its variety of fresh produce, meat, fish, and flowers purveyed by local family vendors made it equivalent in those days to Seattle's famous Pike Place. But it soon disappeared in the wake of downtown development, and in the 90s our sole remaining public market was an eighteen-vendor establishment housed in a World War II Quonset hut, built in 1946 and now rapidly deteriorating. The North Market was less than a mile from our house, and Robin and I had been shopping there every Friday since we moved in. So when the market master invited a group of merchants and regular shoppers to meet and discuss the market's future, we were eager to attend.

Following this meeting, three of us shoppers had lunch and decided to try saving the market. We knew the odds were against us, as they certainly proved to be, but we also thought the family enterprise and culture of the public market, not to mention its fresh food, were worth the effort. Ken Danter ran a full time business, I was now working my way into a new book, and we agreed from the outset that Nancy Duncan Porter would take the principal responsibility. This she did, first of all by recruiting to our effort a judicious selection of merchants, market shoppers, and well-connected people in the city's business community. We constituted ourselves as the North Market Development Authority, and now ensued five years of struggle, 1987-92, to persuade both the city and the merchants to find a new home for the market.

The first and far from least of our tasks was persuading the merchants, who needed first of all to be saved from themselves. For one thing, these often lovable mom and pop entrepreneurs were also crusty individualists unable to work together in their collective best interest. Two years before we came on the scene, the city had given them $50,000 to upgrade the Quonset hut's electricity, heating, and plumbing. But they could never agree on how to spend this money, and legend is that at one of their meetings the 5'8" German sausage maker and 6'4" Swedish apple grower came to blows. So the $50,000 lay in the bank losing purchasing power while the Quonset deteriorated past the point of no return, and the city was quietly getting ready to shut down the market.

As if that weren't enough, the merchants were also suspicious of us as meddling yuppies incapable of understanding their kind of business. Many were second- or third- generation family in this business, and they couldn't quite believe they might be facing extinction. Some dragged their feet the whole way, and here my experience in listening, sorting out the issues, and keeping people focused helped us earn some merchant patience while we tried to persuade the city to give the market another look.

Our first attempts to interest a Republican mayor fell absolutely flat. He was preoccupied with enhancing Columbus's urban culture by sponsoring stock car races through the city's downtown streets, and he couldn't care less about the market. But Nancy persisted with the city planning department, the downtown development organization, the Chamber of Commerce, and the downtown's largest property owner, Nationwide Insurance. Meanwhile we fought off proposals by private developers to relocate the market in whatever out-of-the-way building they happened to own—or, in one instance, to replace the Quonset with an 11-story parking garage and put the market on the roof of the garage.

If not for the next Republican mayor and regular market shopper, we likely would have reached a dead end. But once we had Greg Lashutka's blessing, which Nancy received while sitting in his living room with her newborn baby in her lap, the political wheels began to turn. The Columbus *Dispatch*, before taking an editorial position on investing more taxpayer dollars in the Market, interviewed three of us and asked what this market contributed to the city that its supermarkets did not. My trigger-happy reply was that the supermarkets' chemically grown produce goes from raw to rotten without ever passing through ripe, whereas the North Market's produce offers flavor and texture. But my colleagues bailed me out and rescued the occasion by talking up the market as a cultural institution and tourist attraction, and the *Dispatch* came out in favor of maintaining the market. Then, after who met with whom behind closed doors I will never know, Nationwide Insurance offered to sell the city for $1 a two-story warehouse next door to the Quonset on the sole condition that it be used for a public market. Over the next two years the Quonset was bulldozed, its site turned into a parking lot, and the warehouse renovated by an inspired architect who preserved its ambience and integrity of red brick design.

Now the merchants had to be persuaded to move in and pay higher rents on the questionable expectation of more traffic for their businesses. Some declined, and some new applicants came forward to confront us with a new dilemma. They wanted to establish carry-out lunch establishments serving workers in nearby office buildings, and we feared this would turn our historic market into a fast food court. Here was another poignant new American phenomenon, the advent of upscale carry-out upon the decline of home cooking in a society of two- and three-job families. We wanted more butchers, fishmongers, and produce vendors, but these were not forthcoming, and at last we compromised: you could bring in your sushi or pizza counter if you also devoted one-fourth of your space to Japanese or Italian groceries.

The new North Market has been a sparkling success, with twice as many merchants as the old and the fees from the parking lot paying off the loan for renovating the warehouse. Yet only a single one in each of our prized vendor categories is now interspersed among the bakeries and juice bars, popcorn and ice cream stands, and BBQ, Indian, Italian, Japanese, Kosher, Lebanese, Polish, and Thai carry-outs. But on Saturdays from May through November, two dozen farmers back up their trucks to the market porch and, accompanied by mimes and musicians, offer corn and tomatoes, Swiss chard and asparagus, lettuces and beets, honeys and eggs, berries, peaches, apples, and Christmas trees, almost all harvested within the last 24 hours.

If I hadn't been able in Lima to impeach Dean Countryman by quoting him *verbatim,* or if the new mayor of Columbus hadn't been already a North Market shopper, I doubt either of these adventures would have ended as it did. In Lima everything could have come down to one faction's word against the other's, and the incumbent given the benefit of the doubt. In Columbus we Market supporters might have been dismissed as blind to the realities of today's marketplace, in which the city's billionaire lingerie tycoon gets millions in public funds for a grossly underused 12-lane freeway exiting on to his shopping village, but in which a pittance to support a collective of family entrepreneurs might have smelled too much like socialism.

In both these experiences, the interplay of existing conditions, new departures or resistances, and sheer accident produced an outcome that could not have been predicted, and this echoed what I was learning of Darwinian evolution and marxist historical materialism. Not that the firing of a provincial dean, or the rescue of a public market, can itself be significant for the history of our species or the future of our species being. But these also belong to the everyday push-and-pull through which we create our horizons of existence, and they produce the social space in which our history must find its logic of process. I was soon to learn a theoretical term to explain how this logic can arise from the everyday confusion—"over-determination"—and this ugly word helped me to produce at last the marxian scholarship to which I had long aspired.

6.

I retired officially on June 30, 1991, a week after my 66th birthday, and the English department gave me a big dinner, with speeches by former students and colleagues from across the country, which I was able to hear only with the help of my new hearing aids. Then I sat in on a couple of film courses, swam 40 miles the next February in the university's month-long marathon, and began haunting coffee houses. I'd become enamored of espresso during my Italian summer in the 70s, and then lamented the dearth of coffee houses in Columbus. Now I could walk in any direction and soon sit with my latte to read European history, marxist theory, and the biographies of classical composers.

Over the years as a matter of course I had read biographies of the writers I taught, and that left me with a jaded view of this literary form. Too many of these were stuffed with meaningless detail, and now it was refreshing to read sculpted lives of Schubert or Tchaikovsky where one sees the contour of a distinct personality in active relation to its work and its times. The most moving of these for me is David Cairns's *Berlioz*, which indeed runs to 1400 pages, but only because Berlioz was a giant personality, complete man of letters, and quintessential man of his time who left a huge paper trail from which Cairns selected to produce a masterpiece. His book inspired me to write an article on the structure of *Les Troyens*, the opera Berlioz said he'd constructed according to a "Shakespearean plan." My knowledge of Shakespeare put me in a position to identify this plan, which nobody had yet done, but no scholarly journal was interested in my dramaturgical analysis of operatic form.

Meanwhile, my reading was leading me into a new world of re-thought marxism, and here was another happy accident of timing. The exhilaration of retirement, with all the swimming, reading, and listening to music I now got to do, still left a hole in my life where teaching and politics used to be. I felt fulfilled in those two public activities, and if it weren't for the marxism in I which now immersed myself, I doubt I could have found again the nourishment they had given me. This marxism had emerged while I was otherwise preoccupied, and I could enter a new chapter of life by taking it up at my desk for weeks and months at a time.

In my narcissistic first excitement, I felt as if I'd been waiting decades for somebody else to rescue marxism from its metaphor of base and superstructure without also abandoning its focus on the expropriation of surplus labor. Now any number of people were performing this rescue, and I was electrified by two books published in 1987— just in time for the 1989 Soviet collapse and my retirement—Stephen A. Resnick & Richard D. Wolff's *Knowledge and Class* and Ellen Meiksins Wood's *The Retreat From Class*. Resnick & Wolff follow Louis Althusser in elaborating the concept of over-determination as an alternative to the economic determinism of the base/superstructure metaphor. In denying that society's economic base creates its cultural superstructure in a one-directional causation, they show how both our personal lives and collective history are subject to an everyday push-and-pull of more conflicting influences—political, legal, cultural, and religious as well as economic—than we can sort and weigh. All our explanations must therefore be partial, therefore partisan, and marxist explanations are partisan on behalf of the expropriation of surplus labor. Expropriation may not explain everything, but it explains so much of our species history as to be given a high priority.

Yet this priority can get lost in our effort to disentangle the overall complexity, and, as Ellen Meiksins Wood argues, "the potentially useful concept of over-determination has increasingly become a cover for absolute contingency"—a cover, that is, for regarding our history as a series of random accidents, especially the accidents of discourse as claimed by theorists of post-modernism. Even so, Wood does not reject the concept of over-determination. She proceeds to demonstrate how an underlying logic of historical process works its way up through the crosscurrents of over-determination and explains our progression from slavery to feudalism to capitalism. Her analysis often parallels the Darwinians', above all by showing that this progression was not inevitable: we might have got stuck at various points along the way, and we might yet have to choose between socialism and barbarism.

The paired concepts of over-determination and logic of process spoke not only to my recent political adventures but also to my aesthetic experience as a student of literature. The seedbed from which literature creates its great forms and deep knowledge of life, whether in the tragedies of Shakespeare and Arthur Miller or the comedies of Dickens and Barbara Kingsolver, is a world in whose crosscurrents Hamlet can lose his cool just when he most needs it, or Leah Price can decide to remain in Africa rather than return to a US whose people are blind to the beauty of her tattooed husband and trilingual sons. These literary works depict people trying to live fully the life they've been given, and the marxism I grew up on had no way to engage this life's complexities as revealed in such works. But now a re-thought marxism enabled me at last to join my politics and aesthetics, and the result was a book in which I analyze a baker's dozen of literary works that struggle to represent (or avoid representing) a capitalist logic of process emerging from the welter of over-determined existence.

Writing this book also led me to see differently what I had thought was the place of marxism in my life as a teacher and scholar. I had not obtruded this marxism on my students unless it was relevant to the topic at hand, which it rarely was. But I had also supposed it could eventually be made relevant, and my political and aesthetic interests could be joined, once marxist theory became capable of explaining literary representation in the manner I was now pursuing. Until that happened, I'd always thought, I was just putting my marxism on hold. But I now had to see how even the new marxist theory can be relevant to literature only up to a point. I might be able to demonstrate this relevance, but I also had to recognize how literature's deepest knowledge and power reaches beyond all theory, and how my aestheticism had been all along less integral than I imagined to my political outlook.

7.

After reading a synopsis of my new book, two dozen publishers declined to invite the manuscript for evaluation, and this was by now an old story for me. A decade earlier I'd had the same experience in trying to publish my Melville book, and I've kept as a memento a 1990 letter of rejection for that book. The editor of a respected university press, in sending me his readers' reports recommending rejection, added the following paragraph:

Wishing no longer to give pain to authors so gratuitously and so frequently, I'm retreating into text editing and typesetting—but only because I have no other skills. The academy now seems to me to be full of Savonarolas who, prevented from burning books by their claims to openness to ideas, proscribe the books' publication on grounds of their inferred unfashionableness.

The Marxian Imagination now was even more unfashionable than my Melville book back then, and this time the two rejection letters that went beyond a formula paragraph added that the book sounded original and important but also unlikely to recover the expense of publishing it. They may have been right, and if it weren't for Monthly Review Press's socialist willingness to risk a financial loss for the sake of my argument—once thought to be the mission of university presses—the book would not likely have been published.

The publication ordeal of my books duplicates that of others, by no means all marxist, whose unfashionableness in bypassing the jargons of post-structuralism, post-modernism, and post-colonialism makes them unintelligible to evaluators who are interpellated in these hegemonic jargons. This has not kept some marxists from becoming academic celebrities, but only those who adopt the "post"- vocabulary of "social formation" instead of "society," "subaltern" instead of "worker," "immiseration" instead of "expropriation"—terms that cooperate to banish a concept like surplus labor, with the class theory it entails, from the arena of scholarly inquiry and reflection. We marxists of expropriation might be just as smart, informed, analytical, and "cutting edge" as those who evaluate our manuscripts—studies routinely show the rich getting obscenely richer and the poor more immiserated no matter what else might be happening all over the globe—but they have lost the capacity to hear us.

On the other hand, my experience has been that marxists routinely hear each other. We have among ourselves disagreements and conflicting schools—Althusserian, Thompsonian, and rational choice marxism; postmodern materialism and still base/superstructure marxism. But we are comrades in partisanship against capitalism's systemic injustice and our effort to think through this injustice. When I followed up my book with an article challenging the assumptions of post-modern materialism, the two people whose thinking it criticized most severely were the editor and managing editor of *Rethinking Marxism,* who accepted it without blinking and then introduced it in print with a summary that captured every nuance of my argument.

This book and article were my valedictory to marxism, in the sense that I believe I have contributed what I can to its further advancement. My convictions are as deep as ever, and while I sometimes think of taking up my old Dostoevsky manuscript and elaborating its analysis in the light of all I've learned, this would add nothing more than make-weight to what I've already written. Even so, showing Dostoevsky in *The Brothers Karamazov* to be aesthetically a socialist in spite of himself would give me a lot of personal satisfaction.

What I actually did next was visit Cuba, where Fidel Castro had also become a socialist in spite of himself. In carrying out his revolution, Castro was politically what we would call a liberal reformer. Upon coming to power he said, "I want to make it clear now that I am not a communist" and that the philosophy of his revolution was "humanism and *cubanismo.*" It was only fifteen months later, following the reforms his government introduced during those months, that Fidel acknowledged, "Well, yes, we are socialists." My book argued for a humanist socialism such as he had proclaimed, and Cuba's sometimes bungling, sometimes inspired, trial-and-error effort to create this socialism was something I now wanted to get a glimpse of first-hand.

CHAPTER 7. FROM THE CAPITALIST JUNGLE TO THE SOCIALIST ZOO:

HAVANA, 2003

Since my eightieth birthday I've been beset with insomnia—not my familiar sporadic wakefulness that comes from too much stimulation during the day, but something new and steady that feels more like what Walt Whitman called the knowledge of death. It took me by surprise, and it's a double-edged knowledge—a fear of sleep as the herald of death and an impatience with sleep for shortening the life I have left.

I can remember a time in childhood, maybe just before puberty, when I terrified myself going to bed at night by imagining the earth spinning on its axis for all eternity without me here. Some time later I got up the nerve to ask my father how he felt about death, and he said without hesitating that death is part of life, you can't have one without the other, and that in loving life, he could accept death (more or less) when it came. Death came for him when he was just entering his prime, and this was not only devastating to his family but an insult to his vitality and power of love. Now for almost the first time, I'm trying to learn what he knew then, and it's not coming easily.

Any reader who has come with me this far can see that I am a long-time secular humanist. I don't believe in God, or the immortality of the soul, or metamorphosis or transubstantiation. I think it's ashes to ashes, dust to dust, and reverence for life. But then we socialists are often accused of following a secular religion through which we immolate ourselves in a Cause whose goal is as distant and uncertain as the Salvation promised by other religions. Like the Christians or Muslims who expect human suffering in this world to be followed in the next by reunion with Jesus or Allah, we are mockingly said to expect this world's suffering and sacrifice to be rewarded by happy descendants being serenaded through all time by the buzzing of the bees in the cigarette trees on the Big Rock Candy Mountain where the hens lay hard-boiled eggs. All we're doing, our mockers say, is substituting one pie-in-the-sky religion for another.

But what my father must have understood is that life asks to be lived deeply and that when this happens, when people have had a chance to adventure on life in all the glorious possibilities it offers us, they also have a chance to make peace with death as part of life. We can let go more easily if we have drunk largely of life while also fulfilling some of our talents and desires, and when we acolytes of Marx talk about the free development of each occurring through the free development of all, this is part of what we mean.

I wanted to see Cuba first-hand before I died because the little reading I'd done gave off glimmers of a people steadfast in striving against terrific odds—a monster of an external enemy and a mountain of internal ignorance and groping—to achieve for themselves, their children, and their great-grandchildren the development of each through all. I felt that I could accept death more easily if, besides any sense of personal fulfillment in my own life, I could also believe finally that socialism is humanly attainable. Cuba's long history of exploitation by Spain and the US has much in common with that of all Latin America. But it is also marked by exceptionally frequent rebellions, beginning in the eighteenth century and later inspired by the words of the nineteenth-century national hero, Jose Marti, "with all and for the good of all." Castro's socialism seemed to me more redolent of Marti than of Marx, and I also thought the Cuban people have stuck with Castro through so much thick and thin because they see him for good reason as the heir of Marti.

It would be easy enough to dismiss my claim to have seen Cuba first-hand, since the trip I took in February 2003, with my daughter Rachel and my friend Marlene Longenecker, was for one week on a tour bus with fourteen other people and a 28-year-old guide on the payroll of the Cuban government. At the end of that week this splendid man, Abel Ortega, invited us to return for longer so as to understand Cuba better. He said you have to live there for at least six months, which may be true of any country, and certainly one so dynamic and volatile. But as Henry James also once said, in praising the realism of a British writer whose novel depicted French Protestant youth, the only evidence she had to go on was that she had

> once, in Paris, as she ascended a staircase, passed an open door where, in the household of a *pasteur*, some of the young Protestants were seated at table round a finished meal. She got her direct personal impression, and she turned out her type. She knew what youth was, and what Protestantism; she also had the advantage of having seen what it was to be French, so that she converted these ideas into a concrete image and produced a reality.

I knew what socialism wants to be, and what poverty and ignorance really are. My experience of the university had included some quasi-socialist practice, and I also had the advantage of having seen the impoverishment of life that capitalism is compelled to bring most people in order to enrich it for a few (including me). None of which means that I could see in a week all I needed to see, or that I wasn't seeing through my particular ideological lens, or that I didn't end up seeing what I hoped to see. I say only that my ideological lens was no thicker than everybody else's, and that I felt equipped by long study and reflection to reverse James's novelist and convert the concrete images I saw into perfectly realistic ideas.

We flew to Miami on Valentine's Day, stayed overnight in an airport motel, and lined up early next morning for the inevitable four hours of din and hassle at the airport. Our tour was sponsored by an educational organization licensed by the US government, which qualified us to fly directly rather than illegally through Canada or Mexico, and when our passports, licenses, and luggage were finally processed, we were ushered into a dark basement waiting room, more like a dungeon reserved for Cuban relatives and sympathizers, while our plane was de-prioritized for take-off for as long as was feasible.

After an hour's flight, we passed through long customs lines at Jose Marti airport and were greeted by two guides with their drivers and buses ready to take us to our hotel. There were 28 of us altogether, including a contingent that had flown from New York, and we were to be split into two busloads. We had to choose by next morning which guide we wanted for the week, and here at the outset my hearing impairment produced a double stroke of luck. First, I had to ask Rachel and Marlene that we choose the guide whose English my hearing aids picked up best, and that turned out to be Abel Ortega. Second, the group who wound up in the other bus included a number of Jewish synagogue ladies from New York, one of them born in Havana, whose urgent priority was to find this woman's birthplace and make contact with the city's Jewish community. Liber Martinez, our other guide, accommodated them graciously by abridging the scheduled itinerary, and I would have surely resented this as a time-wasting distraction from the business at hand.

Those on our bus were a varied group, and while we didn't find deep affinities, we soon developed an easy camaraderie. Besides Rachel, the equestrian, and Marlene and me, the English professors, there were a retired professor of sociology with his wife from Massachusetts; a retired high school Spanish teacher from Virginia with his wife who owned a boutique; a New York ballet dancer; a D.C. US government employee; a diehard St. Louis Cardinals fan just retired from Monsanto; a Chicago paralegal; a San Francisco headmaster and wife; and a former Democratic US senator with her two adult children. We clearly didn't share the same political preconceptions, and as the week went on our differences became evident. But we did all seem to share an interest in what makes Castro's Cuba both distinctive and enduring, which isn't its synagogues.

Our week was scheduled as follows: three days in Havana, which included a half-day side trip to a nearby coffee village, Las Terrazas; then a day-long drive to Trinidad including stops along the way, followed by a full day in Trinidad and then a half-day's drive back to Havana for our final day-and-a-half. Days and evenings were mostly filled with scheduled activities, but we also had intervals in which to wander by ourselves, and several of our group rented cars and went off for half- and whole days at a time. This going about independently and talking to ordinary Cubans as you found them was perfectly OK with the Cuban government. But it was technically a violation of the US government's definition of the "educational purpose" that allowed us to be in the country legally. We were not supposed to be lolligagging among the natives or lying on beaches drinking *mojitos*, but to be on that tour bus all day every day getting our education.

At week's end we had a farewell reception and evaluation session in one of Havana's fine old colonial buildings. We agreed while munching our finger food that the tour had been well paced and conducted by engaging and knowledgeable guides. Some of us regretted having seen not enough of X or too much of Y, just as one might expect. But my big surprise was some others who said they were disappointed by Cuba's scruffy public restrooms and boring cuisine. "If you really want to develop your tourist industry," one man said, "You've got to fix up the bathrooms and provide more hot running water." This provoked a sharp response from our retired sociology professor, Hal Jarmon, who'd said little all week but whose show-stopping eloquence now was that if you care that much about tourist amenities, you shouldn't have come to a poor country whose attraction is the spirit of its people and the society they're trying to build. He didn't sound to me political in the way I am political, just sympathetic like Rachel and Marlene and Senator Jean Carnahan, none of whom came home inspired as I was.

I was inspired by my sense that the Cuban people in their labor pains are giving birth to a socialism that enlarges our human nature—and are becoming in that process a historic example that can never be denied. Their Revolution may not survive, but it opens new possibilities for humanity, just like the French and American revolutions—and, like them, it has become contagious. Fidel and Che are revered as heroes throughout the world, and Hugo Chavez launched his "Bolivarian Process" in Venezuela by calling Cuba "a beacon of Latin American dignity."

Yet inspired as I was, I also had to recognize that I could not follow some Americans who emigrate to Havana or Caracas when they retire. Having been a critic of American capitalism for virtually all of my adult life, I have also been one of its privileged beneficiaries, and many benefits it has brought me are what socialism wants for everybody. Having experienced personally so much of what Marx meant by the development of each, I found that now at the end I just couldn't renounce that experience.

2.

The drive from the airport to the Hotel Presidente was a visual shock—small dingy houses on all sides, lots of dust, few signs or billboards, and amidst this dreary expanse a rainbow panoply of ancient cars from around the world going in every direction. I had traveled abroad three times since the war, but not to a third-world country, and the gut-wrench of seeing the structures and infrastructures in which these people live can remind you of the Bronx or Detroit or a West Virginia hollow. (A couple years later Robin and I stayed overnight in Quito on our way to the Galapagos Islands, and its airport outskirts made Havana's seem in retrospect like spiffy suburbs.)

Everyone writes about the Cuban automobile phenomenon, and this too you have to see to believe. Old as these cars might be, body rust is rare. The sun has faded all colors into soft gradations from the black and olive Russian Ladas to the blue Buick Specials, the golden Fiats and creamy Yugos, and the ageless VWs of every size, shape, and color. Some of the tour buses are modest VW vans like ours; others are big sumptuous Volvos, and public transportation consists of three vehicles—motorcycle taxis with a rear double-seat encased in a bright yellow shell shaped like a beetle, 1950s and 60s Buick and Chevy taxis, and not nearly enough Volvo semi-buses whose trailers hold something like 150 people standing room only.

Professional auto mechanics are among Cuba's black market elite, and the antiquity of the cars and absence of spare parts make it easy to see why. But there is also a pervasive do-it-yourself culture of auto maintenance, endlessly inventive and by now a part of the national life. Strolling with Rachel later in our week on the back streets of Trinidad, I saw an oversize 1950s red and cream Ford with its hood up and a man hunkered underneath. I stopped to peer, and he pulled his head out to explain rapid-fire what he was up to. Rachel, being fluent in Spanish, explained that he was replacing his Ford carburetor with a Lada carburetor so as to get better gas mileage. When I nodded in comprehension, the guy gave me a big smile and earnest handshake, as if my interest in his car had made us revolutionary comrades.

At one point, Abel told us, the government furnished a cohort of people with bicycles as an experiment in reducing oil-fueled transportation. But these people burned so many calories pedaling that their food coupon allotments had to be increased, and the trade-off was judged to be wasteful. We did see bicycles, of course, along with mules, horse-drawn carts, motorcycles and scooters, scattered among the Chevys and Ladas. And since everyone who drives a government vehicle is legally obligated to pick up hitchhikers, hitchhiking has become as much a part of the national life as repairing cars with baling wire.

Travel-weary as we were after getting settled in our hotel, it was still early evening, and Rachel suggested a walk. We followed our noses and came soon to the Malecon, Havana's fabled seaside boulevard, where we strolled past adolescent couples locked in hot embraces on the sea wall, toward a plaza far ahead where a music festival was in progress. Rachel told me her surprise and thrill that I'd invited her on this trip rather than, say, Alex, who shares more than she does my interest in politics. I explained embarrassedly how this had been Robin's idea, which I at least had been quick to adopt.

Robin doesn't share my political intensities and wasn't all that interested in Cuba. In fact, she attended her first ever political demonstration—against the Iraq war—during the week we were there. But she knew Rachel had been to Latin America with Joan as a child, and she thought that this week together could be a further step of reconciliation between Rachel and me. Rachel's work as a horse trainer and vaulting coach allows her little time off, and, even with the best of intentions on our visits, we still felt a bit stiff with each other. Now I was in fact apprehensive about sharing a room with her, since she is one of those messy people who travel with a duffle bag indiscriminately stuffed and know where everything is, while I'm one of those organized types with a suitcase full of zippered compartments who forgets where he put everything.

So, big surprise! Rachel didn't insist on emptying her duffle immediately all over the floor, and she was unerring all week long in locating as necessary my dental plate, hearing aids, sun glasses, or room key. Another lingering effect of our estrangement was that I felt tentative about finding an easy tone for everyday living. Rachel is an alert, reflective, and very private person. But we both really wanted this. We loosened each other up with some affectionate teasing, and within a couple of days I felt more comfortably connected than in years, as if now at last as father and daughter, we were acting with all and for the good of all. That stroll on the Malecon was a turning point, and our love has kept deepening since.

Some of what we saw during our week was only casually interesting—a cigar factory and retail shop whose wonderful aromas and elegant humidors reminded me of my El Producto years; a barn-like structure that housed an architectural model of Havana, every street and building of the city in scale, of which Marlene observed drily that it was much less useful than a computer model; and the Institute For Friendship Among the Peoples, housed in a beautiful former embassy, where we listened for an hour to an imposing black woman whose idea of friendship among the peoples was a passionate harangue in Spanish, fragmentarily translated by Liber, about the "Cuban Five" who had infiltrated Miami exile groups plotting terrorism against Cuba. They were caught and incarcerated in the US for now almost five years of solitary confinement without being brought to trial. Most of us were aware of many such US outrages, and there was of course little we could do about this one. From what I could understand of Liber's translation, here was one of those occasions both at home and abroad where I could be grateful for my hearing loss.

Other stops were more engaging historically, culturally, or politically. On our first morning, while driving to our scheduled introduction to the country at the Plaza de la Revolution, we passed Havana's main cemetery. Abel said we could stop here if we'd like, although it wasn't on our itinerary, and we did. This huge cemetery is laid out in a strict grid, with long avenues of vertical sculpture and family mausoleums as living testimony to Spanish colonial graveyard architecture and Spanish colonial wealth. Its opulence of death belonged to the old plantation economy, and it made a sharp contrast with the current national symbol we drove to see next at the Plaza de la Revolution—the famous lighted outline bust of Che Guevara, high up the side of a modern building overlooking the space where Fidel delivers his four-hour speeches to a hundred thousand listeners.

As we were soon to discover, Che is everywhere in Cuba, a presiding presence and patron saint. Easily 95% of the T-shirts sold in the tourist shops are images of Che in endless variety. He is on posters, postcards, photographs, woodcarvings, coffee mugs, and books. In the middle of the country along its main east-west highway is an enormous plaza containing Che's tomb, embellished by a billboard signed by Fidel and inscribed with the words "CHE: Queremos que sean como el." ("CHE: We want you to be like him.")

Images of Fidel, on the other hand, are almost nowhere to be seen. At a barren crossroads on that same highway is a modest statue of Fidel obscured by a clump of trees and very easy to miss. Beyond that, the only Fidel I saw was the one I brought home, a squat woodcarving 2" high and 1" square, crudely painted with a black beard and shoes and a green cap and uniform, holding a wee Cuban flag in a piece of self-mockery mass-produced for the tourist trade. When the six-year-old Evian Gonzalez was welcomed home to Cuba after the months-long furor over his kidnapping by Miami relatives, Fidel was not among the airport throng waiting to greet him, lest he distract attention to himself. A year later, when Evian finished the first grade, Fidel showed up at his school unannounced with a book and a box of candy as gifts.

I think Fidel has come to see himself as an instrument of the Revolution and tries to avoid any cult of personality that might be encouraged by reproductions of his image. Another highway billboard reads, "Fidel, estamos contigo" ("Fidel, we are with you"), a contentious declaration instead of a reified image. Fidel is a speechmaker in an oral society, and his speeches are no longer than Lincoln's in his oral society. (Lincoln's 1854 speech on the Kansas-Nebraska Act runs to 40 small-print pages, and the Lincoln-Douglas debates were all-day tailgates.) The T-shirt and coffee mug images of Che, on the other hand, felt to me like a form of commoditization that doesn't really fit the new morality Che said the Revolution must cultivate. But here are nuances of cultural context that an English-speaking visitor cannot hope to grasp in a week. Che's tomb is un-heroically low to the ground; his illuminated outline bust is on the building of a government agency he once headed; and it could be that the T-shirts and coffee mugs are meant only for romanticizing tourists. In any event, Che's image throughout Cuba is too reified for me.

From the Plaza de la Revolution we were taken before lunch to an outdoor art and music center in central Havana. This occupied both sides of an alley that was closed to auto traffic. Along one side were the muralled rear walls, painted in warm-colored abstract designs, of an entire block of adjacent buildings. On the other side in the middle of the block was a store-front that served as office, art gallery, and DVD shop. I thought the paintings in this gallery pedestrian, and the DVDs on display had no interest for me. In the middle of the alley was an elevated stage with room on three sides for performers to jump on and off, and on the fourth side a few rows of folding chairs beneath an awning for a small sit-down audience. The rest of us stood all around in the sun and took in for an hour some powerful music and dance.

The Cuban people are of every skin-color from the palest white to the blackest brown, and their clothes cover the entire spectrum of colors and gamut of styles. It was as if no two looked alike, and it took me some minutes to see that our performers were not in costume but just being themselves. Their performance began with an African-derived chant sung with haunting depth in a long melodic line by a tall skinny black man accompanied by drum, sax, and bass. Then came the dancers, accompanied by a small band, jumping on and off stage in pairs and threesomes, apparently unaware of each other while immersed in their rhythms and interweaving motions. One could feel the kinesthetic blending of African and Spanish elements that distinguish Cuban music, and this government subsidized cultivation of an indigenous performing art was for me the first high point of our week.

Another came the following night after dinner, when we were welcomed and entertained by a neighborhood chapter of the nationwide Committee for the Defense of the Revolution. We parked our van on an intersecting road and walked around the corner into a narrow dark street with a single light bulb hanging from a wire maybe 40 yards ahead of us. In the dimness we could make out several rows of people and, looping in front of them, some paper-ring chains attached at either end to house lintels. My mind flashed to the Jets and Sharks confronting each other in *West Side Story*, except that here dangling from those paper chains were 8x11 sheets with a message printed in crayon, "Bienvenidos." When we got close, a small, frail-looking, white-haired woman stepped forward and started shaking our hands vigorously one by one, until everybody in both groups followed her lead. She was one co-chair of the neighborhood Committee, and the other was a towering black man who would be a perfect fit on my Pittsburgh Steelers' offensive line and who now delivered in *basso profundo* a sonorous speech of welcome in words I couldn't make out. Three teen-age boys then came out of a doorway with drum, flute, and sax, sat on the curb, and began playing. Then one after another, three young girls in identical costumes of different pastel colors performed a highly stylized dance symbolizing the three deities of Santeria, Cuba's principal folk religion.

This dance ended in my moment of glory. The girl in yellow danced up to me and invited me into the sacred circle. As I saw her approach, my septuagenarian first impulse was to hang back and decline. But I'd once been a decent ballroom dancer, I'd felt the old woman's energy who welcomed us, and I saw in a flash that this was an offer of friendship between peoples and generations that I could not refuse. So I took the girl's hand and imitated her movements while weaving among her partners. This brought loud cheers all round, and when all three girls now beckoned other members of our party, they promptly joined in. The climax came when Malcolm Grant, our New York ballet dancer who'd held back at first in deference to the rest of us, perfectly timed his entry leap and spectacular swirls to now wild cheering.

The Cubans then joined in, and we went on dancing for twenty minutes while some women prepared food, amounting to a second dinner, which they passed around as we broke into groups to talk as best we could—Rachel in Spanish with one woman, Marlene in pidgin with several others, and I in English with a man named Antonio and his strikingly handsome, eleven-year-old son Fidel. Then in all the milling about I found the woman who'd first greeted us and gave her a big hug of *gracias*, and this again brought down the house. Her co-chair ran for the Committee's video camera and made us two oldsters do it again for posterity.

The warmth and transparency of this encounter were for me another surprise that belied what I'd read about the Committee for the Defense of the Revolution as an agency for spying on the populace and ensuring political conformity. There is no way the spirit of this block-party could have been produced by a charade. In something like the full range of their national diversity— Santeria cohabiting with Catholicism and both with secular humanism—these people were responding as unguardedly to us as we were to them, and the candor of their conversation revealed anything but conformity. Also striking was the unaffected warmth with which they welcomed Americans despite our embargo that has made their lives so hard for so long. Friendship among the peoples is not for them an ideological slogan but an earnest yearning. This may be in part because so many Cubans have relatives in Miami, but it was also apparent that their government distinguishes between America's rulers and its people—which could also be a reason why so many Americans find it so rewarding to visit Cuba illegally. My niece Patsy, a longtime Caribbean vacationer who hasn't a political bone in her body, fell in love with Cuba on her first visit. She has returned several times, she sends money to families she's befriended, and I had to think that many of the unattached tourists we saw during our week were experiencing the Cuban people in the same way she did.

It was also the case that members of our party who went off on their own talked to Cubans who were either guarded dissenters or else vocally disillusioned with the Revolution. My well-informed fellow travelers, the former Senator Carnahan and her son Tom, made it a point to go among the people and judge for themselves. I sometimes thought they were making it too much of a point, as if to be sure to see what they wanted to see. But they certainly did see it, and I had to accept their conclusion that at the time we were there, Cuban political repression exceeded any reasonable interpretation of Castro's familiar formula for dissent, "Inside the Revolution, yes; outside the Revolution, no."

Yet for periods both before and after our visit, repression in Cuba has been markedly less stringent, and the government's shifting interpretations of Castro's formula still leave open the long-term possibility of democratic transparency. Even allowing for US hostility, I think this government has been at times truly paranoid, and in repressing dissent has not only failed to cultivate a new morality but also diverted energy from the building of socialism. Even so, it has not lost the loyalty of the Cuban people. At one point the government armed the citizenry and trained them in guerilla tactics for fear of an American invasion, and you don't do that if you fear your guns will be turned back on you. Then, just when Cuba was experiencing a one-third reduction in its standard of living following the withdrawal of Soviet support, the government liberalized the election laws by requiring non-party candidates to be nominated from below and also providing a place on the ballot for voters to mark "none of the above." In the subsequent election monitored by international observers, 99.6% of eligible voters voted although voting was not mandatory, and 7.2% of these nullified their ballots in the manner provided for. This comes to something like an 85% backing of the government in what can certainly be understood as a referendum on the Revolution at one of its darkest hours.

3.

While Cuba's political repression was for me a long-range concern, I was more immediately interested in its effort to build socialism in the teeth of a global capitalism which, if it can be supplanted, must be chipped away at here and there until some tipping point is reached in a future we can't foresee. Like your everyday vulgar marxist, I was more interested in Cuba's base than its superstructure, and on the day leading up to our grand evening dance in Defense of the Revolution, my curiosity had been rewarded by our trip to Las Terrazas, a village of 900 people maybe an hour-and-a-half's drive from Havana. Before the Revolution this had been an isolated coffee village whose terraces are surrounded by a beautiful woodland that includes a small lake, a gorgeous swimming hole carved among the rocks by a tributary stream, and an ecologically unique environment for a broad range of Cuban flora. After the Revolution, the government decided to connect Las Terrazas to Havana by a paved road, and to enhance its one-crop economy with both a tourist installation and an ecological preserve. It now had its own guide, Isidoro, who greeted us in English as we got off our buses and described this laboratory of socialist development while conducting us through the area.

First we passed a woman selling jewelry and trinkets, and then the lake surrounded by woods, with its newly built dock and small boats for rent, on our way up the hill to the village center and school, which were separated by a small plaza. The village center was a barren, L-shaped building that reminded me of a Super 8 Motel. The short leg of the L was an auditorium for town meetings and movies, while the long leg was two stories high with a public telephone, visiting doctors' offices, a beauty shop, a tiny store selling sandals, radios, shampoos, and snacks, and an art studio where people produced paintings, woodcarvings, T-shirts, and scarves before or after doing their day jobs.

Next we were led to the swimming hole, bordered by a hillside grove in which workers were just then constructing gazebos, trails, and benches. Here we all took pictures, and our young ones changed into bathing suits and jumped in. Afterwards Isidoro led us up the terraced coffee hill, above which a motel overlooking the lake was under construction, to Maria's Coffee House. This was the living room of another white-haired woman's apartment, where we sat on wooden chairs while Maria and her granddaughter brewed us coffee and Isidoro explained how Las Terrazas works.

Evidently trying to think globally and act locally, the Cuban government had accepted the need to enlarge the tourist industry as a step toward economic self-sufficiency after the Soviet withdrawal. The island's many beaches were an obvious starting point, and later in the week we were to stay at a lovely beach resort just outside Trinidad. But beaches are more or less interchangeable throughout the Caribbean, and the Cubans also wanted their tourists to come in contact with the island's distinctive ecology and culture. At Las Terrazas there was boating, swimming, and trail walking amidst unique flora, along with local coffee, crafts, and conversation in a bucolic interlude from the more intense pleasures of Havana.

But the marketing of tourism through this model community was also fraught with socialist risk. The coffee growers, crafts people, ecologists, and tourist guides were living side by side while working in very different economies. The ecologists and tourist workers had more formal education, the tourist workers got tips, the crafts people's profits were in addition to their regular income, and the coffee growers' product was more subject than the others' to the price fluctuations of a world market. Isidoro thus had to explain a complicated system of income redistribution in which, for example, the tourist workers were required to return a portion of their tips to the community, not with a view to equalizing incomes for everyone but to rewarding everyone's contribution without also creating capitalism's savage disparities between rich and poor.

I don't know whether Las Terrazas has turned out to be an economic and cultural success in the manner intended. What makes it memorable for me is the manner intended, a blending of individual recognition and reward with the communal ethic expounded not only by Che but also Marti in his "with all and for the good of all." At the time we were there, Cuba was still in the throes of its "Special Period" following the withdrawal of Soviet support. Immediately following 1989 there was a 30% reduction in the standard of living, and during the 90s the average Cuban lost 20 pounds while undernourishment rose nationally from 5% to over 20%. Tourism was thus an economic remedy, yet the tourist industry threatened to produce a two-tiered economy in which people with access to dollars—not only tourist and government workers but also, for example, women M.D.s who the Carnahans were told moonlighted as prostitutes—also had access to a style of living beyond reach for the great majority of people limited to pesos. (At Havana's famous ice-cream store, Coppelia, the line at the peso window was two blocks long and at the dollar window there was no line.) This was a cause of concern and much public discussion while we were there, and over the ensuing years Cuba has begun to de-emphasize tourism and prioritize agricultural self-sufficiency (along with its pharmaceutical and computer industries). Offshore oil has meanwhile been discovered, and this introduces a new set of opportunities and risks for socialist production, appropriation, and distribution..

Here is what I mean by a socialist zoo. Making the economy serve people instead of the other way around, for any group larger than the legendary 150 capable of face-to-face concern for each other's well being, requires a more immediate, shifting, hands-on attention than that of an impersonal market whose single law of profit insures that only a minority can thrive while the majority are thrown an ever-shrinking safety net. The commodified tourism of trinket and t-shirt arcades can threaten the identity and self-respect of any local community, as we see only too well in Cuba's sister islands of the tourist Caribbean. Yet our minds and bodies are refreshed by lying on beaches, and our hearts enlarged by cross-cultural experience, for the possibly greater good of each through all. Cuba has tried to contain the dangers of a level of tourism entailed by the Soviet withdrawal, and who knows but that agricultural self-sufficiency has become newly feasible because of the investment capital provided by tourism? The newly discovered oil, meanwhile, amounts to far less than a dependable long-term resource, and there is no systemic pressure, produced by a fictitious "economy" independent of the people who inhabit it, to drill for more in a Caribbean equivalent to our Arctic Wildlife Refuge. Any discussion of that will involve a lot of humane principles beyond profit maximization.

Abel had said at one point that before 1989 Cuba was living in a "fantasy world." Asked what he meant, he replied that Soviet support had given Cubans a false sense of well being which distracted them from thinking about how to become more self-sufficient. They should have anticipated that this support couldn't continue indefinitely and not been taken so much off guard when it ended. But it seems clear from what I've read since coming home that the pragmatic experimentalism we saw in Las Terrazas was a microcosm of the nationwide effort to make up for lost time—and in that process to heal what Rebecca Clausen, following Marx, calls the "metabolic rift" created by specialized fossil-fuel production of food and other necessities.

While Cuba's economy was in thrall to the Soviets, its state-owned sugar plantations covered three times more acreage than domestic food production, and in exchange for its sugar Cuba imported 60% of its food from the Soviet bloc. After 1989, 40% of the state-owned sugar acreage was turned into 2,000 agricultural cooperatives owned and managed by their 122,000 workers. An additional 170,000 hectares were turned over to individual farmers, with free rent and subsidized equipment, leading many city dwellers to move to the country and take up farming. The government also began subsidizing urban gardening in abandoned city spaces, to the point where 60% of the vegetables Cubans now eat come from organic urban gardens.

This multiform land redistribution was also accompanied by the development of "local nutrient recycling"—worm farms using local cow manure to produce richer humus faster, or cattle feed derived from sugarcane by-products in one mini-climate and from fermented orange rinds in another. Such fine-tuned ecological adaptation depends on the traditional knowledge of local farmers, and of the 105 research papers delivered at a 2006 agricultural conference, 53 were by actual food producers, 34 by research technicians, and a mere 12 by university professors. The "metabolic healing" that reconnects people to the land is also reconnecting mental and manual labor, as if Levin's serfs in *Anna Karenina* had become broad-gauge agronomists just like their master. They are now regularly invited to other countries of the South to explain Cuba's new philosophy and methods.

The socialist experimentation symbolized by Las Terrazas was an inspiration to me and, along with other experiences that week, had me asking myself whether I'd want to be part of all this if my life had gone just a little differently. What if I'd done that 30-year hitch in the army and then retired to Cuba at age 50 on a master sergeant's pension? Or if I hadn't met Robin and had retired from the university at 60? After such a long time of feeling alien as a socialist in my own country, what would it have been like to come here at the end and help build socialism, as some people have done? I'd had a couple years of Spanish in college and probably could have gained minimal proficiency. I might then have been able to participate in common purpose with people I could call comrades in producing the social justice that Buchenwald had mapped into my life's agenda. What deeper fulfillment could such a life have?

But I also had to see that this was not for me a road to have taken. No Berlioz or Stravinsky; no lap pools or Pittsburgh Steelers; no graduate seminars in Shakespearean comedy or undergraduate courses in the literature of oppression; no espresso bars or Asian restaurants; no Henry James. One of my generation's noted literary theorists, Wayne Booth, said we are never more alive than in our cultivated response to works of art. Robin has cultivated in me as well a responsiveness to sport, and I owe the privileged aliveness I feel in responding to art, sport, and so much else to the opportunities given me by my capitalist country. In the socialist world of my dreams, devoted from Day One to the development of each and all, cultivating this aliveness according to affinities would be ordinary for everyone. But in Cuba that will be a long time coming, and I couldn't have gone back now and lived without it.

4.

Eating out three meals a day after years of Robin's cooking, I found the pleasures of Cuban cuisine somewhat limited. Our hotel breakfasts in Havana and Trinidad were sumptuous buffets of fresh fruits and juices, lovely breads and pastries, and eggs cooked to order right before us, all accompanied by fine coffee finely brewed. Lunch was typically a choice of fish or chicken lightly herbed and simply braised, accompanied by a barebones salad and a pudding dessert. One exception was an upscale establishment where servers in elegant uniforms circulated with skewers of spicy meats just off the grill—sausages, pork, beef—each tastily different but taken all together a bit of overkill.

But the big overkill for me, at each and every lunch and dinner, was the inevitable band performing Cuban *son* and concluding each set with *Guantanamera*, composed by Jose Marti and the next thing to a national anthem, before circulating among us to hawk their CDs. As if it weren't enough that music in restaurants makes table conversation impossible for the hearing impaired, not one of the endless *Guantanamera*s I heard could match in cadence, inflection, and lilt the great 50s performances I knew by Pete Seeger and The Weavers. The Cubans may not butcher their song the way our singers do *The Star Spangled Banner* at every sports event, but their tourist renditions gave no hint of the musicality we had heard in the arts alley and were to hear again the night before our departure.

We could buy cocktails before the evening meal, and both Rachel and I fell in love at first sip with the *mojito*, Hemingway's favorite drink and something he got right. Dinner entrees were chicken, pork, or fish as at lunch, only with tastier sauces and accompanied by crisp vegetables and black beans with rice, and over our week I was surprised by the variations in flavor and texture of this Caribbean dish. And our most memorable meal was indeed at a private restaurant outside our Trinidad resort, where the menu was more varied and the cooking more subtle than at the state-owned establishments.

5

We drove to Trinidad on our fourth day, and for entertainment on the road Abel showed us the movie "Strawberry or Chocolate," a beautifully wrought and devastating indictment of Cuban homophobia. When it was over, Abel said simply, "Being a homosexual in Cuba is a very hard task," and we can ask what a sentence like that means by ending on the word "task"—instead of, say, "burden," or "fate." I think it means that where homophobia is pervasive in civil society, as it is in Cuba, an immediate (and easy) task of government is to subsidize films like this in support of gay people who must take on the task of facing down homophobia on the street and in the neighborhood so as to create a living equality. In the US few people imagine that such a responsibility exists. Our first reflex is to legislate equality for each "minority" marked by "difference," then to fight in the courts over this legislation, and meanwhile to leave intact the physical and cultural enclaves in which we segregate ourselves from each other in civil society.

As a matter of fact, I had seen "Strawberry or Chocolate" here at home, and, its incidental flaws being what they are and my ideological irritability being what it is, I had sourly dismissed it as probably financed by Miami's anti-Castro Cuban Mafia. Seeing it again on Castro's tour bus was not at all what I'd expected, and here was another of Abel's ideological surprises.

We also stopped on the way at Che's tomb in its grand plaza on the central highway, and then at the seedy farm town of Santa Clara, capital of Las Villas Province and site of the Revolution's wrecked train memorial. Here in the autumn of 1958 occurred a tide-turning battle in which a trainload of Batista's soldiers, dispatched from Havana to trap Castro and his rebels in the Sierra Maestra, was ambushed and derailed by a heavily outnumbered rebel column led by Che. This cleared the way for the rebel forces to advance on Havana, and three of the train's original box cars, with photographs inside them of Che and his cohort, have been joined at rakish angles to symbolize the derailment of Batista's dictatorship.

Abel then had us make one more stop, which he later regretted, at what had once been a huge sugar plantation. The point of interest here was a very high tower of ornate Spanish architecture from which the overseers could survey hundreds of slaves cutting cane in a field that must have been a half-mile long by a quarter-mile wide. It was a poignant reminder of Cuba's brutal past, and you could understand why Abel wanted us to see it. But it was also here that, besides the clothes and craft sellers we'd encountered elsewhere, we were besieged by women and children begging insistently for money and sweets. Not even the Peter Pan of our group, Jim Phelan, the retired Spanish teacher who charmed Cuban kids everywhere with his sleight-of-hand tricks, could distract these kids from their begging. Abel was taken aback by their onslaught and visibly ashamed. He said these people were guaranteed food, housing, schooling, and health care, so that the poverty they were showing us was a "poverty of the soul" to which he would not expose tourists again.

Another Cuban highway billboard makes a claim which there is no evidence to contradict: "200 million of the world's children will sleep in the streets tonight. Not one is Cuban." The rural housing we saw in and between Santa Clara and Trinidad was dilapidated to say the least. You could look inside an open front door and see in the living room a double bed that served also as a couch, on which three generations of a family might be sitting to watch TV on a 12-inch screen. The walls were bare, except for an occasional crucifix or image of Che (sometimes both), and their paint was faded inside just like outside, where you also saw people sweeping with crude brooms and washing with mops and buckets. Drab and worn as they might be, all had roofs over their heads and freshly washed clothes; there was no litter in the streets, and almost everybody seemed diligent to do what cleaning they could.

During the "Special Period" Cuba couldn't afford either to produce or to import paint, but it did provide access to computers for all its schoolchildren. Most of us knew before we arrived that literacy, health care, and sport were the Revolution's three great priorities, and that UN studies show Cuba's literacy, infant mortality, and life expectancy rates to be markedly better than the rest of Latin America's. All that had played a part in making us curious to come. We had seen in the streets of Havana, as we were to see again the next day in Trinidad, classes of uniformed schoolchildren being taught outdoors or else on field trips. Abel now explained also that here in the countryside there were no school buses since they would be impossible to fuel, but that rural people thought nothing of kids walking miles to school and that in some places there are schools with only seven to ten students, equipped with TVs and computers. In rare instances where any school is too far to walk, the government provides individual families with a home computer and a visiting teacher.

Our beach resort outside Trinidad was nicely designed and landscaped, with a large outdoor swimming pool just a few yards from the sea, a thatched-roof bar with lounge chairs adjoining the pool, still more lounge chairs on the beach, and then, of all things, a two-story bank of sleeping rooms with bath that would make a Super 8 Motel look luxurious. After finding our cells in this block, we changed into swimsuits and escaped to the beach, where after a swim I stood knee-deep in the water talking for an hour with Malcolm Grant. He was a charming man maybe in his late thirties, originally from Oklahoma and now a Broadway dancer. He'd been to Cuba before and was returning to deliver ballet shoes donated by his Big Apple friends to the national dance company and its satellite academies. Malcolm shared none of my political identification with the Revolution, and in fact began with some sharp criticism of the government for its niggling support of the dance company. But I also had a sense he was feeling me out politically, just as he was about his being gay, and while I showed my politics to be far left of his, I also didn't blink at his sexual orientation. We liked each other, and what also struck me as our conversation meandered was his admiration for the Cuban people. He especially admired the pedagogy, discipline, and style of their dance company, for whose Havana performance he had got us tickets for the night before we were to leave. In all of this he reminded me of my niece Patsy.

That evening our entire two dozen-plus ate at one big table in the private restaurant just outside our resort, and our fine meal was followed by a discussion, chaired by Malcolm, of how much to tip our guides and drivers for their week of serving us so well. Some proposed customary percentages for tips, while others wanted to add more in sympathy for the Cuban people's ordeal— although it wasn't always clear which ordeal they had in mind, enduring the US embargo or enduring Castro. A small minority, including Rachel, Marlene, and me, wanted to tip the drivers the same amount as the guides, in the spirit of Che we had seen so many Cubans trying to cultivate. But this idea was rejected by our majority, and after Malcolm passed his cowboy hat the first time to collect for the dinner check, he passed it again for the tips we finally voted on.

Rachel took part in this discussion with the same quiet assurance that had been disconcerting me all week. She was often the one who knew where people were and rounded them up for the bus. She had asked directions and translated as necessary, she had persuaded the others to tip our Las Terrazas guide Isidoro, and she had drawn our bus driver Luis from the margin into the circle by asking him about Cuban music. She'd been discreetly attentive to my doddering, and her arguments on the tip question were incisive and cogent.

I mostly missed out on my children's growing up, and a second price I paid was not noticing when they *were* grown up. A second price they had to pay, in case growing up without a father weren't enough, is how long it took me to see them for who they are. Unconsciously for me they were still kids, as if no time had passed since our first separation, and now here comes Rachel, a national board member of her professional association, persuading her elders and drinking me under the table with *mojitos* when I thought her drink was Shirley Temples. A floodgate was opened in me, and perhaps only now have I really awakened to the competence and wisdom of all my three children.

6.

Founded in 1514, Trinidad is Cuba's third oldest community and a UNESCO World Heritage Site. Its architectural heritage is represented principally by the cathedral in the town's main plaza, where we sauntered next morning amidst a class of kindergarteners learning songs and two Volvo busloads of European tourists. This building's proportions and distributions of space were among the most beautiful I have seen anywhere, and while it had the same worn look we had seen in Havana public buildings, it was also undergoing renovation thanks to UNESCO. On the morning we were there, a workman mounted on a very high scaffold was filling cracks in the plaster of the dome, applying his socialist labor on behalf of his neighbors' Catholic devotion.

In Havana a couple of days earlier, on the side altar of a church, Marlene and I had seen hand-scrawled notes, with accompanying lit candles, thanking Jesus or Mary for finding the writer an apartment. So here was another ideological surprise. If ever a religion were the opium of the people, it has to be the Catholicism that cultivated ignorance and superstition among the native peoples of Latin America while also acquiescing in (or abetting) their mass murder. But here the Cuban government, even if with UNESCO financing, was respecting its people's Catholicism just as it does their Santeria. We tourists walked silently through the cathedral among dozens of communicants kneeling in prayer.

Next to the cathedral was the Museo Romantico, exhibiting 19th century household furnishings, a collection of china, and an eclectic variety of pieces none of which cried out for attention. What struck me the most here was the novel being read by a young woman sitting outside at a card table to collect our admission fee: *Jane Eyre* in Spanish. From the museum we then sauntered through town for an hour before our *Guantanamera* lunch, and then we visited a clinic and were addressed by the M.D. on duty.

This barren establishment reminded me of the 84th Field Hospital sixty years ago. It was indeed a building and not a tent, with thin interior walls separating patient wards, examining rooms, and the nursing station. But it was even so the next thing to a tent: there was neither furniture nor decoration around the cots in the ward, nor much equipment visible in the examining rooms. The doctor explained how everyone gets free health care and a clinic like this is a first stop for the rural sick. If their illness cannot be diagnosed and treated by procedures and medicines available here, which apparently doesn't happen too often, they are sent up the chain to more comprehensive hospitals in other locations.

We asked him about Cuba's policy of segregating people being treated for AIDS, which is widely considered a human rights violation, and he said that Cuba regards it as a public health measure parallel to European and American segregation of t.b. patients when that disease was rampant. He said that AIDS patients were not mistreated, that their medical care could proceed more efficiently if conducted in one place, and that the spread of AIDS could meanwhile be slowed while they were recovering. One of our group also told him what we'd heard about women M.D.'s moonlighting as prostitutes, and asked whether he or M.D.'s he knew felt tempted to supplement their incomes in the dollar economy. He replied with the same thoughtful transparency that impressed me so much in Abel, taking the question with complete seriousness and thinking out his answer as he spoke. He said doctors were paid more than other people, certainly enough to live on, and that the M.D.'s he knew felt the same obligation he did to use their spare time learning more medicine. If some were moonlighting for dollars, he thought they were being irresponsible to the nation's investment in their education. He didn't use words like Abel's about "poverty of the soul," but I think he had the same moral idea of what it means to become like Che. Or as Cuba's great public intellectual, Jose Antonio Blanco, had put it a few years earlier,

In my case, we have about seven people in our extended family. We face the problems that all Cubans have been facing— sometimes we can't get soap, we can't get toothpaste, sometimes we don't have cooking oil. But it's unthinkable for us to face the crisis through stealing or prostitution or leaving the country—we face the crisis with collective principles.

Our next stop was at a local office of the national Federation of Cuban Women, and what struck me immediately here was the physical space itself. There were pictures on the walls, an ancient typewriter surrounded by papers on a desk, more papers in sorted stacks on another desk, and pamphlets scattered about. We had seen nothing like this in Cuba, but it was warmly familiar to me—just like Ohio State's first Office of Women's Studies. When Women's Studies was launched as an academic discipline, the women who began it found pictures for the office walls, along with lounge chairs, lamps, and whatnot, without waiting for the university to provide these amenities. Their feminist sense of purpose created an immediate material ambience, and here at a World Heritage Site I felt this same ambience.

The handsome director of the women's federation who now addressed us in halting English wore a sexless, un-picturesque, ankle-length dress, unlike most Cuban women in their miniskirts but just like the Ohio State women back then. She summarized Cuba's progress toward gender equality, and then all my hearing could make out of her answers to our questions was that domestic violence had been eliminated from the countryside. This left us incredulous, and from what I could tell, here was the one Cuban we'd met who was mouthing a party line. Abel had told us that only 30% of Cuban couples living together are married and that this 30% has the fourth highest divorce rate in the world. The *machismo* that prompted a movie like *Strawberry or Chocolate* must also have contributed to establishing the Federation of Women, and although we had seen any number of strikingly self-possessed women, it also seemed a stretch to suppose that domestic violence had been uprooted from the countryside. *Machismo,* in any case, as we were to see two nights later in the fable performed by the national dance company, is still very much at issue in the country of *son.*

On Friday morning we began our last full day on the island with an early start from Trinidad and the obligatory stop to pee and shop on the highway back to Havana. Here was a scaled-down version of the service areas you find on American toll roads. A building on one side of the toilet house was the gas station and store. There you could buy snacks, souvenirs, and clothes, and one counter was devoted to a bizarre assortment of auto parts: one tire in each of three sizes, a couple of odd wheel rims, assorted oil cans, horns, and Lada carburetors. On the other side was an outdoor bar under a thatched roof featuring rum drinks, soft drinks, ice cream, and light fare. We toileted, bought a soft drink, and browsed in the store, where I bought Robin a carved frog and myself a Fidel-style shirt to wear while writing like right now.

We got back in time for lunch in Havana Vieja, the city's old section near the harbor, and then were left on our own until the farewell reception and critique scheduled for late afternoon. When Rachel and I came to the big outdoor book market, I had another surprise—not that the books on offer were overwhelmingly works of political theory but that these were almost entirely classics by Marx, Lenin, Trotsky, and Mao that seemed to me only marginally relevant to the history being made here. Cuba's socialist laboratory escapes all familiar marxisms, and I wondered how buyers could find much reading on these tables that might help them in what they are trying to do. Having made their Revolution, and now searching for what Jose Antonio Blanco calls a "humanistic socialism," the Cubans are in a path-breaking process that goes beyond Lenin, Trotsky, and Mao, although one can easily imagine how they might be inspired by those thinkers. Even so, I wished they were reading more literary works like *Jane Eyre* and *King Lear*, and theoretical works like *Knowledge and Class* and *Democracy Against Capitalism*, from which I've drawn so much of my socialist conviction.

But in some of these impressions, as it turned out, I was a victim of the country's deceiving appearances for the superficial visitor. We had seen two sparsely stocked bookstores in Havana, both disappointing. One was a Barnes & Noble *manque*, with overhead signs indicating different categories of books in different floor areas, but only a handful in each category and a lot of empty shelf space. The other had fuller shelves, with used books as well as new, but an equally random inventory. Only later back home did I learn from informed people that those shelves were bare because Cubans grab up books immediately wherever they are available and what we'd seen in those bookstores was simply the residue. Havana's annual book fair, where both Cuban and foreign publishers display thousands of titles, attracts hundreds of thousands and disrupts bus service for the entire city. (I've also been told there was a time when medical students demanded that neurology textbooks not be sold without an ID because they were gone before the med students got to them.)

On weekends in Havana Vieja there is an outdoor artists' market featuring paintings, pottery, crafts, clothes, and jewelry. My shopping so far was well under the US's allowed maximum, and I was ready to leave a few more dollars in the local economy. But although a couple of parodic paintings really appealed to me (especially one of Andy Warhol's Campbell soup can), I didn't want to deal with the logistics of getting one home and finding wall space when I did. So I contented myself with a knit sweater as a gift for Robin's sister Tracy, over which Rachel offered to bargain with the woman in Spanish. Her asking price was $25, I said offer her $22, and she replied no, $25. She then explained softly that this was a fair price based on the time and skill she had put into the work, and it was the only price she would accept. Embarrassed for having failed to be like her in being like Che, I paid her price, and Tracy loves the sweater.

Then we bought a soft drink and asked a sad-faced woman sitting at a table overlooking the sea if we might join her. She smiled and said "si" through her missing front tooth, and she and Rachel began immediately to talk. It turned out she had a university degree in astronomy, a child and no job, and she explained how, grateful as she was for her education, Cuba now has more educated people than jobs to fit their learning. I thought back to Abel's statistics about the divorce rate, since this woman looked too worn to have a partner she could care about, and also to those stories about women M.D.'s. Rachel and I separately were tempted to offer her money, but also afraid of insulting her forlorn dignity, and when we finished our drink we didn't linger.

7.

By now I needed an afternoon nap and left Rachel to continue wandering while I was whisked to the hotel in a motorcycle taxi revving along the Malecon. It was a breathless ride, with the driver chattering loudly in broken English above the motor and I wishing I could hear him. When Rachel got back, we proceeded to our farewell reception with its complaints about Cuban bathrooms, and from there to the Gran Teatro de la Habana in the city's hotel and entertainment district. Here we had time for a sidewalk *mojito* before the dance performance for which Malcolm had got us tickets, and while sipping her drink Marlene came down with food poisoning from the afternoon reception and had to miss the performance. I also succumbed by the time we got back to the hotel that evening, and we were both totally miserable—headache, nausea, diarrhea— for the next day's flight and layover in Miami, the following day's flight home, and our first days back in Columbus buried in its foot of snow.

But that dance performance in the Teatro's main auditorium, the "Sala Garcia Lorca," was another high point in our week. The auditorium was filled with Havana's multi-colored, rainbow-clothed people, and the "Fabula Cubana" mimed by the dance was how a young man from the countryside leaves his dear old father to make his way in the city. There he meets his destined antagonist, the most flamboyant, be-jeweled terpsichorean of *machismo* you can possibly imagine, surrounded by a bevy of adoring women in fabulous costumes. Behind them on a moving platform is a band whose brass sonorities, woodwind inflections, and Stravinsky-like off-rhythms fill the whole theater with tremendous energy. The two men's opening dances, the city dude suavely showing off his repertoire while the country bumpkin gets off completely on the wrong foot, were performed with a combined athleticism and refinement that I have seen only in the choreography of Stravinsky's friend Balanchine. Then the dances of the *corps de femmes* as the band motored across the stage behind them were similarly disciplined and spectacular, and the story reached its climax when the country rustic unbelievably out-danced the city slicker and won all these doting women.

I shudder to imagine what Garcia Lorca might think of this fable performed under his nameplate, let alone our Trinidad spokesperson for the Federation of Cuban Women. But then what fable would you have—of a *campesino* Stakhanovite furiously swinging his machete so as to exceed his sugar cane quota? a single mother astronomer staring sadly out to sea while striving to be like Che? a Sierra Maestra *Billy the Kid* featuring Che derailing a train? The Cuban composers, choreographers, and performers, like the Cuban homosexuals in their hard task, were starting with the culture they've inherited, and while it could be only my wishful thinking that they were mocking this culture as a step toward outgrowing it, they were surely raising to a new level the indigenous performing art we had seen in the muralled alley a few days before.

Here again, in art and culture as in economics and politics, the promise and fragility of the Cuban Revolution are two sides of one coin. With food, housing, literacy, and health care underwritten for all, the Cuban people have at least an opportunity to think of becoming like Che while they are also in the process of becoming a nation unto themselves. Under Castro's leadership, says Richard Gott, the noted historian of Cuba, "the Cuban people 'stood up'...and understood for the first time who they really were." Their self-understanding did not come in a bolt of lightning that illuminated stone tablets brought down by Castro from a marxian mountain top. Castro came to marxism through the same erratic process by which his people came to understand who they are, and the commandment he gave them was to cultivate Che's morality in support of Marti's politics—"humanism and *cubanismo.*" Their persistence and loyalty in doing this work, in trying to establish a personal and political life "with all and for the good of all," is one reason why Castro remains a world-historical figure at 85, just a year younger than I in my idle reminiscing, despite the effort to destroy him and re-colonialize his people pursued by ten US presidents who have passed into oblivion.

Not that I think the Cuban Revolution has already succeeded, or is by any means certain of success. Its mistakes have been costly but not fatal, and its next generation will no doubt make mistakes that could still become fatal. But as the dying Ralph Touchett says to the still struggling heroine, Isabel Archer, at the end of James's *The Portrait of a Lady*, "I don't believe that such a generous mistake as yours can hurt you for more than a little," and the fundamental generosity of Cuban socialism has proved to be contagious. Hugo Chavez's "Bolivarian Process" in Venezuela is redolent of Marti and Che, and it shows signs of infecting a postcolonial continent.

But if I came home inspired, it was not by Cuba's influence on others, nor by its material and cultural accomplishments. What Cuba showed me indelibly in the flesh and blood of its endearing people is that we are not creatures of a narrow, unalterable "human nature" that limits us to dog-eat-dog competition for just the barest chance to live our lives fully. We are creatures instead of a capacious and flexible "species being," which enables us not just to dream of full lives but also to find ways to live them, by all and for the good of all.

Abel Ortega, in all of his twenty-eight years, epitomizes for me this struggle to produce a new life. His forthrightness, transparency, and discrimination—"Before 1989 Cuba was living in a fantasy world"; "Being a homosexual in Cuba is a very hard task"; "The poverty of these people is a poverty of the soul"—belong to a people who not only think it possible to become like Che but are also thinking their way through this labor of becoming. Abel in his Cuba made me long for my parents, those team players and lovers of life, who I know would have been inspired as I was.

It must then be said also that our capaciousness as species beings allows us to accept life at its meanest, and to dumb ourselves down enough to embrace this meanest as inevitable—every creature for itself in the ideologically contrived jungle of the marketplace. Rosa Luxemburg said that humanity must choose finally between socialism and barbarism, and the recent history of America shows many signs of a latent barbarism that would not surprise my old army buddy Phil Epstein. Now at the end I also must question whether the America I first fought for with Phil, and then studied with love for a lifetime, can remain an object of faith and a beacon to the world as it was for so long. If socialism does beat out barbarism, it will likely be in spite of us Americans, and something that now doesn't surprise me is how many recent thinkers, none of them marxists, argue that the American Empire is in terminal decline parallel to that of the Romans and British. Which of course doesn't mean that socialism will prevail in the world, or that our beloved nation will have lived historically in vain. Yet whatever might or might not happen, Cuba has put it for me finally beyond doubt that, as another billboard on its main highway proclaims, "Un mundo mejor est posible."

ACKNOWLEDGEMENTS

David Frantz first urged me to write this, and I would never have done it without him. Our years of working together were among the richest of my life, and only my respect for his judgment led me to attempt something I would not otherwise have dreamed of. Dick Altick seconded David by urging that my personal history as a GI Bill Jewish radical who became a literary critic and academic activist was "virtually unique of its kind." Terri Paul kept encouraging me in our rests between swimming laps, and she followed up by turning her novelist's eye on my chapters and suggesting every kind of improvement. Jim Phelan added to that his discrimination as a theorist of narrative in a series of priceless suggestions for becoming a better storyteller. And my keystone reader was David Terry Paul, acolyte of Milton Friedman and master of mockery, who forgave me my Marxism for the sake of a higher cause.

Jim Kincaid has been reading my manuscripts for decades, and again he brought to this one the whole piñata of his incisiveness, sarcasm, and love. Robin Bell Markels is my court of first and last appeal, and she was at first very skeptical of this project. If my first chapter hadn't made her a convert, I would never have had the courage to go on. Once I did, I had sturdy support from my sister Mimi Harris and my dear friend Bob Jones, whose historical writing I have shamelessly pilfered. Yet none of all that help could have come to this fruition without Gordon Grigsby and Barbara Bergmann, who were eager to publish the book at *Evening Street Press* when nobody else would, and whose editorial advice and devotion to design surpass anything in my previous experience.

For almost two years, whenever I sat down to write these pages I was distracted by pain from arthritis, stenosis, and three herniated lumbar disks. After trying every alternative before turning finally to surgery, I was rescued from a smug bone mechanic by two scholars of the spine, Dr. Josue Gabriel and his assistant Jennifer Kibbey, whose knowledge, skill, and humanity gave me back a life in which I could keep on writing. I could never thank them enough.